LEADING
Naked

UNPLUGGED | UNEDITED | UNFILTERED

MONA VOGELE

First Edition, 2025
Printed in the United States of America

Published by The Mojo Dept.
MAV Six Zero, LLC dba The Mojo Dept.
ISBN Publisher/Imprint: The Mojo Dept.
Library of Congress Control Number: 2025915543

Hardcover ISBN: 979-8-9994539-1-4
Paperback ISBN: 979-8-9994539-0-7
eBook ISBN: 979-8-9994539-2-1

Cover design by The Mojo Dept.
Interior design by The Mojo Dept.

This publication is intended for informational purposes only. The author and
publisher make no guarantees of success and disclaim any liability arising
from the use or misuse of this book.

For rights, permissions, or to throw digital confetti:
info@monavogele.com

Library of Congress Cataloging-in-Publication Data
Vogele, Mona.
Leading Naked: Unplugged | Unedited | Unfiltered / Mona Vogele. — First
edition.
pages cm

ISBN 979-8-9994539-0-7 (pbk.)
ISBN 979-8-9994539-1-4 (hardcover)
ISBN 979-8-9994539-2-1 (ebook)

1. Leadership — Psychological aspects.
2. Business — Personal development.
3. Emotional intelligence.
4. Authenticity (Philosophy).
I. Title.

HD57.7 .V64 2025
658.4'092 — dc23
2025915543

This book is dedicated to my family — my rock and my inspiration. You've grounded me through gut-punches that knocked the air clean out of us, the victories so electric they left us reeling, and the "what-the-hell-now" curveballs that never stopped flying.

I've watched you fall, then rise — again and again. And somehow, in the middle of it all, you taught me the only weapon we've ever really needed is love. Not the polite kind — the bear-hug kind that hijacks the room and dares the darkness to try again.

For every storm we've walked barefoot through — dodging potholes, patching scrapes, and flipping off the detours — you proved that leading the way isn't optional in our family. It's in our DNA. It's a call we answer because we don't know any other way.

Forget the airbrushed leadership summits — I got my real training woven into the fabric of our lives: group texts, late-night calls, and kitchen-table "pass-the-mashed-potatoes-and-here's-a-life-lesson" moments that hit harder than any keynote ever could. Every page of this book doesn't just thank you — it immortalizes you as the training ground that forged me into something unbreakable.

This one's for you, my marvelous, perfectly imperfect tribe.

Bow your neck...

Table of
Contents

The Invitation

PART

01

THE SIX NAKED TRUTHS

PART

02

INFLUENTIAL LEADERSHIP: THE FULL REVEAL

The Uprising

The Revelation

Leadership isn't staged — it's bare-knuckled, unyielding, and defiant: standing up, stripping down, and declaring, "This is who I am. This is what I stand for." Shatter the illusion. Destroy the armor. Step in naked, with nothing to hide and nothing to lose. Because the world doesn't need another PowerPoint messiah or assembly-line boss. It needs a raw, unfiltered revolution. Leaders scarred into steel — not faking it for likes.

— Mona Vogele

The Invitation

LEADERSHIP LAID BARE

"Leadership isn't a title—it's influence that shapes the future. Step up and own the revolution."

MONA VOGELE

Shattering The Illusion

Let's not pretend. You didn't crack open this book because you were thirsting for another leadership yawn-fest or craving a room-temperature shot of "best practices." You saw the word naked and thought, "What kind of beautiful madness is this?"

Good. That means you're not asleep at the wheel. And that little twitch of curiosity? It's the gateway drug — the first hit that gets you hooked on tearing down the façade we've all worn and some of you are still clinging to like it's bulletproof.

Now, before you start clutching your pearls — this book won't land you in HR for streaking through corporate. **Leading Naked** isn't about shedding clothes; it's about shedding the act — exposing truth and torching the corporate cosplay. We've been marinating in leadership dogma for decades — charts, checklists, and a conga line of core values so empty they could moonlight as elevator music. And the worst part? We swallowed it like gospel and asked for seconds.

That ends here.

This is your manifesto for embracing the evolution you're about to undertake — for dropping the pretense and tossing out the tired playbook. This book isn't whispering affirmations from a yoga mat. It's a brick through the glass ceiling. A sledgehammer to business-as-usual. Your best friend handing you a shot of tequila and saying, "Let's flip the table and wreck some comfort zones."

Your weapons cache? Six naked truths. You've met them — they've been hanging like wallpaper in conference rooms for decades, but rarely are they lived. Rarely are they felt. And almost never are they used together like the holy sextet they are. Until now.

So here's the warning: if you're hunting for safe, this ain't it. This is a blind leap into realness — with nothing but grit and guts to catch you. Leading so fiercely, so authentically, the world can't help but look up and say, "Now that's someone worth following."

This isn't a journey. It's a jailbreak. Cross this line and you don't get to unsee the mirror. You're here to lead like a seismic event, not a footnote.

So — if you're ready — let's strip it down and crank it up. Because when you truly lead naked, you don't just step into the room — you tap into the electricity of the people in it.

Unleadership

Imagine you're in the front row at the kind of concert that rearranges your circuitry. The bass isn't just thumping — it's resyncing your heartbeat. Every chord? Hits like a war cry straight to the chest. That's what leadership should feel like. Not sanitized or scripted. Just raw and real.

> Unplugged.
> Unedited.
> Unfiltered.

Leadership done right isn't some committee-approved cha-cha with paint-by-number steps and polite applause. It's a sweat-drenched, speaker-shattering uprising — the kind that leaves the floor scorched and the crowd changed.

When the six naked truths at the heart of this book stop playing solo and start colliding, you don't just get growth — you get a full-blown awakening. This isn't about sprucing up your "executive presence"; it's about yanking the cord out of the amp, going full acoustic, and making the whole damn room feel you. It's about leading like your soul's onstage — with zero plans to play it safe.

We're not here to sit quietly coloring inside the lines — we're crowd-surfing over fear, slamming down on impostor syndrome like a kick drum, and setting your inner critic on fire with an encore it never deserved.

Each chapter — its own power chord. Each theme — its own spotlight. And don't expect clean breaks; this isn't a corporate org chart. It's a messy jam session where trust echoes through every riff, accountability shadows the stage, and emotional intelligence plays basslines you don't notice until they're gone. That's the point — life isn't compartmentalized, and neither is leadership.

So throw on that metaphorical leather jacket and crank the volume. Because this? This is your soundcheck. But before we blast into the setlist, we've got to ignite the stage with raw, unyielding purpose — the kind that flips every decibel into direction.

Purpose Lit — Drive Loaded

Forget perfecting an off-the-shelf, neatly packaged "success formula" from some stale blog post. Strip it all back — title, clout, prestige — and get to the only question that matters:

"Why do you want to lead?"

Not the LinkedIn answer. Not the one you trot out in interviews. The real reason. The fire-in-your-gut one that sparks even when everything else is telling you to quit.

We're not polishing bios or stacking gold stars. This is about tunneling through the noise until you hit bedrock — the immovable reason your feet stay planted when the easy exit looks sexier than a four-day weekend mainlining espresso martinis, and nobody would blame you for bailing.

Because when all hell breaks loose — when sales implode, morale flatlines, and the quarterly numbers bleed red — survival doesn't come from a playlist full of motivational bangers. It comes from instinct. Conviction. And a purpose that refuses to go dim.

So don't chase someone else's dream or lead because somebody stamped you with "potential." And definitely don't do it because you think it'll look baller on a future résumé. Greatness wasn't born to be formatted in Times New Roman. The only thing that matters is what refuses to stay quiet — the hunger that won't let you walk away.

Why do you *really* want to lead?

Say it out loud. Write it on the wall in Sharpie. Tattoo it on your brain. This is your compass — your North Star when the road ahead looks like doubt, deadlines, and dysfunction.

And once you've got your "why," watch the "how" crash through the walls like it's been waiting for you all along. You'll start seeing cheat codes everywhere, patterns will shift, and the world begins to bend in your favor.

But don't stop there — your why is just the fuel. Drive is what burns it, and it doesn't wait for inspiration. It moves. It surges when you're underestimated. It keeps showing up long after motivation has packed its bags. And when you're flat on the mat, bleeding doubt, your drive refuses to quit — still spitting in the face of surrender.

Maybe your why is building the chances your younger self never got — or refusing to repeat the toxic playbook you inherited. It could be carving a new path for future leaders. Or maybe you're just done worshiping average — and everyone still clinging to it. Whatever your why, it's your drive that keeps it alive.

So yes, lock in your why. Then slam that sucker into gear and don't look back. Because that's the kind of dangerous the world needs.

Unmasking Influence

Here's what only a few gutsy voices will tell you: leadership is not that complicated. It never was. But dress it up in jargon, force-feed a few frameworks, slap a premium price tag on it, and suddenly people are paying thousands just to be told, "Hey, don't be a jackass."

At its core, leadership is influence — untamed and undeniable. It doesn't beg for titles, org charts, or permission slips. It takes the stage mid-set, drowns out the noise, and makes the crowd lean in. It's gravity with stage lights — inescapable, pulling people into its orbit before they even know what hit them.

But here's where most people go wrong: you can't wield influence while hiding behind a mask. The real thing doesn't live in curated, "look at me, I'm crushing it," highlight reels. It breathes in the unarmored, sweat-on-your-shirt version of you — the one that feels too exposed to show, and yet is the only one worth showing.

We're drowning in filters. Addicted to likes. Confusing attention for connection and calling it progress. We've built empires on image — hollow cathedrals to vanity — while the raw presence that actually moves people rots six feet under.

Sure, on the surface, you might rack up cheap applause. You might even trend for a minute. But it's the real you that leaves a residue — the kind that lingers long after the room empties.

Right now, the world doesn't need more algorithms — it needs truth-tellers. People willing to lead us out of the bottomless, scrolling graveyard of dopamine addiction and designer loneliness. Social media promised us community and handed us curated isolation. We ghost each other in plain sight, pretending to be seen while starving for belonging.

We don't need another social media influencer. We need someone real enough to lead like an unplugged set — no filters, no Auto-Tune. Just magnetism so fierce it shakes the dust off our humanity. Leaders with skin in the game. Leaders who give a damn. Who'll fight to bring us back to each other with a kind of hope that won't vanish with the next software update.

The so-called secret to success? There is no secret. Only one undeniable reality — the one the world keeps ignoring but can't silence forever:

> Humanity is the cause.
> Connection is the rebellion.
> Leadership is the revolution.

And like it or not, you've already been drafted.

The Battle Cry—Leading Naked

Influential leadership is gloves-off gospel—a stand against apathy, ego, and the soul-sucking safety of the middle lane. It doesn't settle. It doesn't sanitize. It burns through the excuses that keep leaders weak. And it never hides behind the label of "soft skill." It's showing up full throttle and swinging hard. No stunt double. No backup plan. You're not here to parrot recycled leadership clichés. You're here to make legacy mean something again. All you need are the six naked truths—your leadership arsenal, the only weapons savage enough to lead the fight:

Trust is the foundation—where influence begins.
Connection is the current—fuel with purpose.
Communication is the frequency—cutting through the noise.
Emotional Intelligence is the lens—depth with a soul.
Culture is the ground—you own it, or it buries you.
Accountability is the anchor—where truth holds steady.

Six truths. One mission—to build something that actually matters. We've got enough spectators. Enough keyboard commandos posting hot takes from the sidelines. Enough wannabes chasing fame like it's purpose. What we need are leaders with mud on their boots, truth on their tongues, and steel in their chest cavities.

And make no mistake—we're leading in a time when division is currency, when tearing down gets clicks and building something real makes you look like a relic. When staying safe is applauded and standing firm is seen as radical.

But guess what—courageous leaders burn through the static and build anyway: teams, companies, communities, futures worth handing to the next generation.

And here's the thing — these leaders don't discriminate. They show up when no one's watching, when everything's on the line. In boardrooms, sure. But they don't stop there. They show up on battlefields and at kitchen tables, in classrooms and faith spaces, in the forgotten shadows of our society — alleys, shelters, prisons, recovery circles — wherever leadership dares to call them.

So, wherever your leadership calls you, be relentless. Be unshakable. Be the kind of leader whose humanity shakes the room and leaves stories they'll never erase.

Our battle cry?

We're **Leading Naked — Unplugged, Unedited, and Unfiltered.**

We're not here to perform. We're here to transform. No bravado. No BS. This is where the mask comes off.

- → The illusion? Torched.
- → The stage? Ours.
- → The impact? Unstoppable.

This is leadership stripped to its core — unfiltered truth that doesn't whisper, it calls you by name.

And this is your invitation. Not to watch history from the sidelines. Not to wait for permission.

To answer the call.

Are you in or out?

THE SIX NAKED TRUTHS

CHAPTER

Naked & Unstoppable

STEPPING FEARLESSLY INTO LEADERSHIP

"Leadership's not about knowing all the steps—it's about dancing like a fool, owning the rhythm, and daring others to groove along with you."

MONA VOGELE

Two Left Feet, Finding The Beat

Alright. You've got the new office chair, a title that sounds fancier than it feels, and a calendar stuffed with meetings that pretend to matter. Welcome to leadership — where every move you make is either setting the tempo or setting off alarms. You're either the game-changer or the ghost story they'll tell new hires.

First-time leadership? Oh, honey. It's not some gentle onboarding with a smooth glide into greatness. It's a faceplant with surround sound and an audience close enough to hear you drop an F-bomb without a mic.

I still remember my debut. Fresh off a short-lived college attempt, armed with exactly zero street cred and a backpack full of ambition, I was dropped into the deep end. No floaties. No map. Just grit, adrenaline, and — truth be told — panic.

The team? More sitcom cast than strike team. I wasn't leading — I was dodging landmines with a laminated lanyard. And strategy? Please. Every decision felt like entering nuclear launch codes with sweaty hands and a Magic 8-Ball flashing, "Ask again later."

But the real body blow was still warming up in the bullpen. Because apparently, the universe wasn't finished screwing with me. Turns out I wasn't just stepping into a new role — I was replacing Linda.

The Linda. The immortal Office Mom. The credibility-building, peace-brokering, plant-growing unicorn of a person who somehow made leadership look like a warm hug and a Pixar movie rolled into one. Her people didn't just respect her — they were ride-or-die loyal.

And now? They were mine.

Jake: An IT virtuoso. The guy could rebuild a tech stack before lunch, fix the office Wi-Fi on his coffee break, and still flex as a JavaScript wizard — think Sheldon Cooper with better people skills.

Sarah: Marketing wizard with a lethal design instinct and wildfire energy that can't be contained — dropping concepts that ricochet through any room she enters.

Greg: Hawaiian-shirt-wearing sales hurricane, cracking jokes like a stand-up comic utterly unacquainted with "inside voices." Loud. Unmissable. Probably his own genre of human.

And then there was me — fumbling, trying to conduct this blended orchestra while they silently wondered if I'd lost the sheet music.

And for the record? I had.

Finding My Rhythm

Thank God for my parents. No sugarcoating. No participation ribbons for breathing. Just blunt-force, kitchen-table gospel:

> *"Don't kid yourself — you can't lead squat until you know who you are and what hill you're willing to die on."*

Back then? I had no clue. No plan. Just nerves, caffeine, and a half-buried instinct that kept dragging me back to the one place that never demanded a résumé — music.

I'd spent years learning how to drop into the groove, ride out dissonance without blinking, and recover mid-beat like I meant to crash there. And then it hit me — I'd been welding the scaffolding for this all along. Hell, I'd been training since the days of hairbrush microphones and mirror arenas, convinced I was born for Madison Square Garden. Every wrong chord? Just another rehearsal. Every stumble? An encore in disguise. I wasn't prepping for perfection — I was building calluses for the main stage.

Turns out leadership doesn't live in some one-size-fits-all package. It lives in your own rhythm — pulsing with untamed wildness. The kind that doesn't ask permission to hit hard, break weird, or wail loud.

Sure, some leaders are classical — buttoned-up, locked down, every note sanded down until it shines. Not a hair out of place, not a beat out of line. And in certain arenas, that flawless precision is the whole game — think corporate ballroom dance, where missing a step could cost you the title. If that's your lane, own it. Precision takes guts.

But some of us? We're jazz with torn edges. We don't follow a set score — we hijack it. We ride the pulse of the room, bend the rules until they squeal, and hit the notes nobody saw coming. We riff like we've got nothing to lose. We crash like cymbals in a crowded bar. And then we recover — louder, rawer, and with a grin that says, "Yeah, I meant to do that."

But knowing your rhythm? That's just the start — it's the pregame stretch before you light up the stage. The real magic kicks in when you strap swagger to that beat and swing like the whole room's holding its breath. Crank it until the walls hum. Let the imperfections snarl right through the mix until they're unmistakably yours — the kind of calling card that stops people mid-scroll and makes them chase the source.

So what's your rhythm?

Copying someone else is a rhythm-killer. Stop it. Step up. Crank your voice until it rearranges the furniture. Your people aren't camped out for flawless — they're here to see if you've got the guts to lead when the spotlight burns hot and there's nowhere to hide.

Leadership Swagger: No Strut, All Signal

When it comes to swagger, it's not about stomping around like some relic from a '90s Wall Street fever dream. That chest-thumping, loudmouth, "look-at-me" bravado? It's dead — buried six feet under next to fax machines and floppy disks.

Real swagger doesn't shout or beg. It charges the air. It's voltage, not volume — walking in like gravity just shifted. The kind of presence that doesn't need a mic drop — just the silence after you speak stalking the room. No mask. No borrowed lines. Just you, and everyone suddenly remembering who the hell they are because your authenticity punched through their excuses.

With that kind of confidence, the room doesn't just look — it locks in. Eyes track you. Energy snaps to attention. Before they even realize it, they're leaning in, feeling it in their bones like a bassline they can't shake. That's the switch. You stop being background noise. You're not on the agenda — you are the agenda. Not the warm-up act, but the headliner they showed up for.

The twist? You're not the boss in this story. You're the host. You cue the music, pack the dance floor, and hype the crowd until they find *their* rhythm. You don't hog the spotlight — you build one so big, everyone standing near you starts to glow.

That rhythm and swagger? That's your leadership signature. Your signal in a world full of static — cutting through the corporate fluff dressed up as titles and hollow speeches. The one that makes people stop and say, "Yeah… that's the one. The real thing."

And your signature can't be mimicry. If it's not yours, it's worthless. Make no mistake — if they can swap you out and no one notices, it was never your signature leading. You were just office décor with a name tag.

You've got your own sound. Your own frequency. Your own knockout groove no one else can replicate. Stop dialing it down. Stop remixing yourself to fit someone else's playlist. Make it yours and crank it until the walls vibrate.

Then go deeper. Because that "signature" isn't just a vibe or a style — it's the surface-level trace of something deeper. The identity beneath the volume knob. And when that identity snaps into place, the signature stops being cute and starts being undeniable.

So that's where we're going next — into your identity. The part of you no one can fake, steal, or copy.

The Signature Source Code

Grab a pen. Yeah, a real one. Not your phone. Not Google Docs. We're going old school because typing feels too safe — and this exercise? This one's supposed to shake something loose.

Now, write down your top four or five core values.

But hold up. If you dare write "teamwork" or "innovation" or any other bland-as-oatmeal executive cliché, tear the page in half and start over. This isn't for show. This is your mirror. And it only works if you're mercilessly, unapologetically honest.

I'm talking about the stuff that punches you in the gut when the world goes sideways. The truths you can't mute, no matter how much your pride begs you to. The beliefs you'd throw hands for — especially when no one's watching. ***This is soul-level territory.***

You can imitate every LinkedIn guru or corporate darling on the planet — and still end up as nothing more than a leadership hologram. But when you lead with a signature stamped by the values hard-coded into you? People feel it. They move with it. They believe it.

The most magnetic leaders I've ever met weren't polished. They were rooted — in who they are, what they stand for, and the silent certainty they carry the moment they enter a room.

> So stop scrolling.
> Stop performing.
> Start digging.

Ask yourself: "Who the hell am I?" This isn't a branding exercise. This is your operating system. Your core wiring. And if you need help, think archetype.

 **The Hero?** The one who doesn't just push forward but drags fate behind them because courage isn't a concept; it's how you breathe.

 **The Creator?** The visionary. Builder of what's next, wrecking ball to what no longer serves, with zero need for anyone's permission.

 **The Rebel?** Born to shred the handbook, burn down the system, and build something bigger and bolder from the ashes.

These aren't the only archetypes; you can check out the rest later. But know this — no list of labels on the planet will tell you who you are. That's your excavation. The archetypes are just a mirror, helpful for spotting patterns, giving language to the instincts already in you. Use them to figure out who you are, then drill down into what you actually value. Because values aren't strategy — they're your inner compass, born from lived experience.

Now, you don't need to define them all today. In fact, you don't even need full sentences yet. But you do need to start.

> What truly fires you up?
> What pisses you off?
> What hill would you die on even if no one followed?

That's the raw material you want. So dig. Then keep digging. Get to the marrow — the non-negotiables that whisper (or scream) when you're ready to fold. Don't overthink it. Don't try to pick the "right" one. Just feel the pulse — your rhythm. Find *your* source code — that unmistakable part of you. Then build on it.

The Bedrock of Legacy

Forget what you've heard — leadership doesn't come in some shrink-wrapped corporate mold. It's wild and unscripted. No formula. No guaranteed path. Just instinct, nerve, and the audacity to keep moving when the lights flicker and the crowd goes silent.

That kind of leadership? It's not built on trends. It's built on the six naked truths — six essential forces that show up again and again in every leader who doesn't just manage but moves people. Six truths that start as weapons of survival — raw, essential, and sharp. Your naked arsenal for every room you walk into, every decision you make, every standard you set.

Keep them in play and they harden into something else. Every time you lead with them, lean on them, sharpen them, they sink deeper. They become bedrock — the invisible architecture beneath your voice, the bassline driving every bold vision, every hard conversation, every move that hits with impact. This is the kind of leadership that doesn't just show up — it flips tired systems and leaves a mark that won't fade: intentional to the core, fearless in the moments everyone else sidesteps, and relentless in a way that refuses to break long after the noise dies down.

So here's what's next: we crack them open. Quick. Clear. No static, all signal. What you're about to learn sets the stage — the real show comes later. So take a breath. Roll those shoulders back. And let's turn it up.

Naked Trust

Trust. It's the price of entry for leadership. Not the flimsy, head-nodding, "Got it, I'll follow up" knockoff kind that breaks on impact. I'm talking about the kind that makes people lock eyes, link arms, and run headfirst into the fallout together — not because they have to but because they believe in you that much.

Real trust is the lifeblood of influential leadership. It doesn't just level you up — it straps a cape to your back and turns average into unstoppable. Without it? Even the slickest teams fold faster than a paper straw in a frozen margarita.

What no one really says out loud — because, well, common sense should cover it — is this: trust doesn't come shrink-wrapped in an onboarding packet, and it sure as hell isn't earned just because your email signature flexes "Big Boss Energy."

Trust is built in moments, not memos. It shows up when it costs you something, when the timing sucks, and when every excuse is begging you to bail. It's defined by the behind-closed-doors decisions no one sees, the public ones no one forgets, and the way you own them all when the spotlight hits.

That's when people decide. Is this someone I'd follow into the blast zone? Or someone who disappears when the ground starts to give? That's the price. Pay it — or stop pretending you're leading. Because if you won't make the call, take the hit, and stand in the consequences, don't expect anyone to follow you anywhere — least of all into the fire.

Sounds brutal? Good. Now let me show you how I learned this the hard way — on day one.

The Starting Line

Rewind to my rookie leadership moment — if you can even call it that. The setting? My first team meeting with Jake, Sarah, and Greg. The vibe was straight out of a Western showdown (cue the theme from *The Good, the Bad, and the Ugly*). Everyone eyeballing each other like someone was about to pull a metaphorical six-shooter. The air was so thick with skepticism you could spread it on toast.

I knew I couldn't stroll in, throw down a PowerPoint, and expect them to suddenly trust me. That's not how it works. Trust is earned. And the catch? It's slow as molasses — like a cowboy pouring a shot of whiskey during a tense saloon stare-down. Deliberate. Nerve-wracking. Impossible to rush.

So I did the one thing that scared me more than pretending to have it all together: I showed up as a full-on human. Not "Boss Me" with the bullet points and buzzwords — just me.

I didn't just open that meeting —I threaded it through with honesty: my obsessive love for music, my loud, lovable family, the time I face-planted over a mic stand during a big-deal presentation (yes, there's photographic evidence —and no, you can't see it). Even my kryptonite, chocolate chip cookies. Because nothing says I'm human like carbs and vulnerability.

Did I know if it would work? Not even slightly. I was winging it like an overcaffeinated bird flying straight into a wind tunnel. But here's what I've learned from fearless leaders and full-send entrepreneurs: they don't waste time plotting every move in advance. They lead by making the right call in the moment —especially when the outcome's a giant question mark.

Once I cracked the door to trust, I realized something: this was just the starting line. If I wanted to build something real —something that could stand when things spun out —I had to go bigger. Trust was the concrete slab. Now it was time to stack stones until it sang like a cathedral with a heartbeat.

→ And the first stone? Connection.

Naked Bonds

I'm not talking about meaningless "Nice job!" drive-bys, limp-fish handshakes, or smiles so manufactured they should come bundled in packs of ten. That's not connection. That's a cardboard cutout version of connection —flat, lifeless, and not fooling anyone.

Real connection is gritty. It's earned in the trenches —when the deadline's circling like a vulture and your team's one Slack ping away from flipping desks and rage-quitting life. It's human.

And getting there isn't glamorous. It's a dance — but don't cue the rom-com soundtrack. Think more middle-school slow dance: sweaty palms, shifty eyes, and absolutely no idea where to put your damn hands.

> You'll fumble and catch the stares.
> You'll overstep and feel the sting.
> You'll wonder if everyone's just pretending to like you.

But then an unexpected moment hits — something shifts. A truth blurted out so raw it makes someone spit coffee mid-revelation. A shared screw-up; a moment so unguarded it rewires the room.

And just like that — walls drop. Rhythm syncs. And now? You're not just herding people toward a deadline. You're leading a crew that's in it with you. Fists up. Shoulders locked. All in. Because true connection? It's rarely pretty.

But make no mistake — it's powerful.

The Awkward Beginnings of Connection

Take my first team. On the connection front, a glorious mess. Less rock band, more unfiltered open-mic night where no one knew the song, the key, or who handed Greg a microphone.

Meanwhile, there I was — freshly minted "leader" — spinning chaos like a rookie DJ praying the track wouldn't skip, one meltdown away from Googling "leadership exit strategies."

So what did I do? What every panicked rookie does: I reached for the most cringe-worthy Hail Mary in the corporate playbook — yep, you guessed it, team building. The kind of forced-fun fiasco where the only bonding is over shared trauma.

Specifically — pictionary. With the theme of *team synergy*. Let that horror sink in. Office jargon as stick figures. Blank stares. Spirit-crushing silence. And me, internally screaming while my dignity quietly packed a bag and left the building. A slow-motion pileup of confusion, secondhand embarrassment, and emotional evacuation.

Then — salvation. Someone blurted the obvious: "What are we trying to do here?" A pause. A crack. Then a snort-laugh (full confession, that was me). And just like that, the silence shattered. We were laughing. Hard. Not the fake, office-approved "ha-ha-nice-one, Jake" laugh — the ugly, gut-level, oh-my-God-we're-finally-human kind of laughter.

And right there — in the wreckage of badly drawn bar charts and busted icebreakers — we became something more than coworkers trying to survive a Tuesday. We were on our way to becoming a crew. Not bonded by brilliance but fused by the mess. By the cringe-soaked moments where the armor finally fell off. Because that's where real connection starts: in the shared humanity that emerges when nothing's working — and you show up for each other anyway.

Listen Before You Lead

That wreckage moment slapped me awake. Real connection doesn't come from scripted charm or TED Talk intros — it comes from showing up fully and listening like the verdict's already in and you're the one on trial: every eye locked on you, every silence screaming something you'd rather not hear, and every casual "you good?" being graded in real time.

And I'm not talking about that performative "uh-huh, yeah, totally" crap we all fake while mentally praying to the Outlook gods for a meeting cancellation. I'm talking about the shut-the-hell-up-and-listen kind of listening — laptop closed, phone facedown, not leaving until the truth drags up a chair across from you.

So I stopped trying to "fix" my team and started asking questions that cut past the BS and cracked something wide open.

> What lit them up — *really* lit them up?
> What made them want to throw their desk out the window?
> What made them human?

Turns out, the truth wasn't buried — it was sitting at the table, draped in quirks, caffeine, and the quiet audacity of being real.

Jake? His silence wasn't detachment — it was sniper-level precision. Give him space and he delivered brilliance with no wasted motion.

Sarah? Her energy wasn't chaos — it was a tenacious drive to kill boring and build what the rest of us were too scared to imagine.

And Greg? Greg was a confetti cannon of enthusiasm. He didn't need to be tamed — he needed to be aimed.

None of it — *and I mean none of it* — had a thing to do with deadlines, dashboards, or whatever "team synergy" is supposed to mean. (Still don't know. Still don't care.) This wasn't about aligning KPIs. It was about aligning with them.

The moment I stopped managing and started connecting? Everything changed. Not in some preplanned twelve-month engagement strategy. It shifted like a stadium crowd in the bottom of the ninth — bases loaded, full count — when the kid just called up from the minors rips a walk-off grand slam into the night.

 **You want a team that connects?** Stop performing — start leading. Not just when it's easy or safe. Go first — when it's messy, before the perfect words show up. That's the job. Leaders don't wait for trust and connection — they build them out loud and in real time.

And yeah — it's hard. It should be. Because titles don't make you a leader. Your people do. They're the receipts. The reflection. The proof of how you showed up — when it counted and no one else would.

Naked Communication

Building trust and connection is one thing. Strengthening them? That happens in the pressure cooker we call the daily grind — never through watered-down pleasantries. Comfort builds nothing; pressure transforms. That's when communication steps in and starts cutting deep — not with hollow gestures or HR-approved feedback forms but with verbal crowbars powerful enough to pry open stuck doors and slice through a bloated inbox of fake emojis.

Real communication builds bridges. Fake communication builds resentment. Anything less than bold honesty? That's just a dress rehearsal for failure that sucker-punches you into reality.

From Encryption to Connection

Take Jake — our in-house tech sorcerer. The guy could reroute satellites in his sleep and make it look easy. Brilliant, sure. But his updates read like a quantum physics manual written in Elvish —

and when one person holds all the knowledge, it's no longer leadership; it's a cult with Wi-Fi.

So we adapted. We launched our very own decoder sessions. Once a month, Jake hit the whiteboard and shattered the language barrier — no tech-speak, no ego, no "dumbing down." Just straight-talk. Not to box him in or "people-person" him into submission, but to rip down the wall between expert and everyone else.

Once we cracked the space open, something shifted. People didn't just nod and zone out.

> They leaned in.
> They asked questions.
> They got curious.

And Jake? He wasn't just some wizard behind a curtain anymore. The ideas weren't just his — they became ours. Loud. Shared. Powerful.

No More Pretzel Wars

Then there were Sarah and Greg, our sales and marketing dream team — or so we thought. Picture two street vendors screaming over how to sell a giant pretzel. Same mission. Same product. Zero harmony.

So we reset the stage with biweekly strategy sessions. At first, it was pure theater — polite smiles, stiff nods, and fake peace colder than a break room fridge. A collaboration charade. Everyone playing nice while guarding their turf.

So we stripped it back. Dragged the elephants into the open. Called the turf wars for what they were — torching the illusion that their supposed alignment was anything other than rivalry in disguise.

And the results? They hit fast.

> No more silos.
> No more idea-hoarding.
> No more "my win vs. your loss."

Once the walls dropped, it was shared goals, shared metrics, and shared accountability. Slowly, the rhythm changed. Greg's loud shirts, Sarah's chaotic brilliance—no longer distractions. They became the groove that made ideas come to life. They stopped tripping over each other and started building something together. Not fighting for the spotlight but designing one big enough for both to shine.

→ The wins? Felt like all-hands victories.
→ The losses? Lessons they dissected together.

That's what real dialogue unlocks: momentum, mutual respect and a team too busy building the future to waste energy guarding territory. And the old pretzel wars? Replaced by a full-on buffet. Bigger table, bigger wins, and nobody left hungry.

Deny the Wobble, Own the Collapse

Corporate communication—the art of saying nothing with too many words. And building anything from it? Think IKEA bookshelf: parts missing, instructions unreadable, and your partner twirling the Allen wrench like a baton at halftime. Everyone's frustrated, no one says it, and you're ready to light the whole thing on fire just to take control.

If you're not stopping to name the gap and figure out why the shelf keeps leaning, you're not building anything real. You're stacking kindling and praying it doesn't collapse mid-quarter.

An honest exchange of ideas isn't burying people in a year-end report and hoping everyone's too bored to ask questions. It's the moment someone says, "Okay, that sucked — now how the do we fix it?"

→   Awkward? Absolutely.
→   Frustrating? Like folding a fitted sheet.

But that's the point. It'll make you squirm, expose skeletons, and force you to face facts you'd rather ignore. Because real communication lives in the tension. In the silence after the truth drops. In the moment someone finally says, "I have no idea what we're doing, but I want to figure it out." That's the heartbeat of a team that's still alive.

So yeah, the comparison holds: communication is the IKEA bookshelf of the corporate world. Looks simple on the box, but brutal if you ignore what's holding it together. Miss that and you're building blindfolded — faking certainty and leading a team one wobbly leg from collapse the moment real weight hits. And if you don't catch the wobble, you can't stop the fall. That's where awareness steps in.

Naked Awareness

Emotional Intelligence — EQ, if we're shortening it. And yeah, I know. It sounds like something you'd skim past in the self-help aisle, right next to *How to Hug Yourself into Success*.

Roll your eyes if you want. The fact is, it's the soul of leadership. It's the current running through your influence. The energy that separates leaders who move people from the ones who just manage schedules and slowly suck the life out of the room.

Without it? You're presiding over a slow-motion exodus — your team vanishing into the Bermuda Triangle of disengagement: frustrated, foggy, and one bad video call away from checking out for good.

I learned that the hard way — up close and unprepared.

When I first dropped into leadership, I didn't know jack about emotional intelligence. I thought it meant standing taller, speaking sharper, outpacing everyone in the room — even if their résumés read like mini-epics and mine felt more like a first draft.

So I overcompensated. I spit-shined the mask. Walked in like I had it together, all veneer and strategic one-liners. I looked the part. I even fooled people into believing it. But inside? I was flailing in a leadership costume — shiny on the outside, empty on the inside.

What I eventually learned, after the posturing cracked, is that emotional intelligence isn't a skill at all. It's a state of being. It's not a box to check — it's the emotional wiring, the awareness behind every decision, every conversation, every moment that actually matters.

Leadership has never been about having all the answers. That's a myth sold by people who never led anything worth sacrificing for.

It's the core-deep understanding that it's all about people. It's the part of you that sees behind the poker face, that hears what didn't get said, and reads between the lines before resentment starts writing its own story.

It's about reading the room without a spreadsheet, knowing when to push, when to hold back, and when to shut up and just be there. It's building a space where people can show up as who they truly are — and know it's safe to do so.

EQ is the line between leaders who transform and those who stall out. It's leadership at its most brutal — and its most beautiful. You don't need to fix everyone, but if you can't see what's real in them, you've got no business leading them.

Wrecked and Rebuilt

Forget the slide decks and coaching seminars — my crash course in emotional intelligence was leading three people who already knew their worth; I just had to catch up. There was no manufactured structure to prop me up — nowhere to fake confidence or bluff my way through. Just three wildly different individuals who wrecked every lazy assumption I had about leadership — and rebuilt me from the inside out. They challenged my blind spots, pushed me past every easy answer, and forced me to see leadership in an entirely new light.

> **Enter Jake:** precision thinker, fiercely his own man. Independent to the core — he didn't crave attention, only respect.
>
> What did I do? I did what insecure leaders do — I micromanaged. Not because I doubted him, but because I hadn't earned his trust yet. I smothered his rhythm with "helpful check-ins" that, to him, felt more like a chokehold. And shocker — he shut down. Not for lack of skill, but because I wouldn't let him own his brilliance.
>
> The second I backed off and let him run his lane? He didn't just deliver. He went full throttle and left scorch marks in his wake.

The Lesson: Sometimes the right move is getting the hell out of the way.

Then came Sarah — a live wire wrapped in creative genius. Think brainstorms at the speed of caffeine and ideas that struck like thunderclaps.

My rookie instinct? Contain it. Put up fences. "Guide" her creativity into tight little tracks. Bad call. She didn't need a filter — she needed fuel. Once I stopped boxing her in, she lit the place up with genius you can't contain.

The Lesson: Don't leash the lightning. Hand it a bigger sky.

Cue Greg. A one-man pep rally in human form — enough energy to short-circuit a small city. My knee-jerk reaction? I tried to dial him down, worried he didn't "fit" the corporate mold.

Wrong. Greg was culture personified — the frequency that made our team feel like a team. What I saw as "too much" was the team's mojo. Just because someone doesn't look like leadership doesn't mean they aren't leading.

The Lesson: Don't mute the magic because it doesn't wear a tie.

These three? They proved emotional intelligence isn't about molding people to fit your style — it's adjusting yourself to understand theirs. It's choosing connection over control even when your ego's begging for the wheel. Because the second you quit playing sculptor and start playing student, compassion takes the stage — and leadership stops being an act and finally gets real.

The Compassionate Edge

Jake, Sarah, and Greg didn't just open my eyes — they split them wide and shoved me straight into the reality of EQ.

Yeah, leadership is about reading the room — but more than that, it's also about feeling it. It's noticing when someone walks in carrying invisible weight, the silence in their "I'm fine," the energy shift that says something's off.

In those moments, real leaders don't wait for a scheduled check-in. They slam the brakes, look that person in the eye, and say, "I've got you. What do you need?" That's not just kindness — that's compassion with teeth. It's seeing the human before the hustle.

You want absolute loyalty? Start giving a damn when it's inconvenient. You won't find that in your *Leadership 101* handbook — but it should be in the first freaking chapter, written in permanent ink and underlined with a blowtorch.

And if you think compassion makes you soft, you're already too brittle to lead. Compassion is the lever that gives you a real advantage, separating leaders worth following from glorified middle managers posting quotes they don't live by.

So stop performing leadership. Show up human. Drop the act and meet people where they are — not where the org chart says they should be. Embrace the unpredictable craziness that comes with leading humans. That's where leadership grows a soul.

And that soul? That's what births culture. Not the framed values. Not the annual kumbaya. The real thing — culture with EQ as its backbone.

Naked Culture

Building an influential culture isn't about plastering empty slogans on beige drywall. Real culture lives in the bones of the people who'd crawl through glass to keep it alive.

It's the raw, visceral sinew that keeps the human machine from falling apart when the plans implode and your team's juggling deadlines, drama, and enough caffeine to jumpstart a dying star.

It's not fake smiles or corner-office role-play — it's connection, conviction, and the courage to show up *all in*. That rare chemistry — the kind of shared charge that makes people stay late because they believe, not because they're scared.

You can't fake it, roll it out with cupcakes, or duct-tape it back together after a bad quarter. Culture is alive — it's the electricity running through everything. When it's strong, it powers the mission. When it's weak, it blows fuses and kills momentum. And when it's toxic, it doesn't just stall progress — it burns the whole place down from the inside out.

And just in case you didn't know: it starts at the top — with you — and bleeds into every "WTH?" moment, every tough conversation, every fist-pump victory. It drives the team forward, sets the unspoken rules, and dictates the pulse in the room. Ignore it and culture won't wait — it'll write the story without you.

Unclaimed Ground Gets Conquered

Know this — you already have a culture. Whether you've built it with intention or left it to form in the shadows, it's alive. Breathing. Evolving.

And if you're too busy polishing excuses to take control, trust me — someone else will happily hijack it for you. They'll whip up their own version of what "works" — and make no mistake, it won't look anything like the masterpiece in your head.

When leadership goes dark, teams don't sit idle — they improvise. They invent rules. They decide what flies and what fails. Sometimes it limps along. Most of the time? It mutates into a twisted mess of cliques, whispered complaints, and "that's not my job" energy. They stitch together their own ecosystem, complete with values and dynamics that make sense to them, not to you. Fragmentation, misunderstandings, and petty drama don't just happen; they grow in the absence of a clear, intentional culture.

Never forget — culture doesn't wait for permission. It's forming right now, with or without you. Step back from it and you're handing the keys to something shapeless — and probably toxic — that will quietly build its own throne and start calling the shots.

Velocity over Vibes

Building a thriving culture isn't just part of your job as a leader — it *is* your job. You're the architect. The anchor. The living proof of what's sacred — and what's not.

The twist? Real culture doesn't come *from* you — it's shaped *by* you and strong enough to outlive your presence. It shows up in the moments you can't script or control — the force that holds when everything falls apart. And if it can't breathe without you, it's not culture — it's a codependent circus propped up by your shadow. Step out, and the tent collapses.

Get it right, and you've got something bigger than a vibe — you've got velocity. The kind that builds loyalty on autopilot, fuels creativity like jet fuel, and turns average contributors into synced-up assassins who break records instead of punching clocks.

Of course, mediocre cultures can coast along — but legendary ones dominate. So don't just preach it. Commit every day to:

Building it.
Backing it.
Living it.

And to make sure it lasts, it can't just feel good. It needs a spine made of steel. Culture doesn't live in a mission statement — *it lives in the choices you make.*

In what you tolerate.
In what you reward.
In what you refuse to let slide.

Because culture without accountability? That's just a glittery house of cards. It'll sparkle right up until the first gust of reality rips it apart — fast, ugly, and under the unforgiving glare of everyone who thought you had it handled.

Naked Ownership

Accountability — the dreaded word people whisper somewhere between performance reviews and postmortems like it's some ancient curse. The fact is, it's the great equalizer — the callout that strips the armor off every "I've got it handled" pretender in the room. It's the muscle that doesn't flinch when the wheels come off and excuses start flying like shrapnel. And no, it's not finger-pointing or pretending a calendar full of one-on-ones makes you a hero.

Real accountability is standing dead center in the blast zone and saying, "This mess? It's mine. And I'll fix it." No spin. No sidestep. No soft language to dull the edge. Because when you take real ownership — public, uncensored ownership — you tell your team that mistakes aren't death sentences. They're launchpads.

That kind of ownership? It's the unsexy superpower that separates the sleepwalking teams from the all-in warriors. It's not glamorous, but it's gold.

Ego or Eat It

I didn't learn about accountability from some overpriced seminar with catered lunches. I learned it the way most leaders get schooled — from that first team that refuses to play along with performative leadership. They didn't care about my prepackaged plans or rah-rah rhetoric. They cared about whether I'd own my mistakes without derailing everything we were building. And believe me, I made mistakes. And every time? I had two choices:

1. Double down on my ego and pretend nothing cracked.
2. Or step up, eat it, and fix what I wrecked.

Both get remembered — one as a story worth following, the other as the punchline everyone else learns from.

Your call.

Owning the Wreckage

Let's not dress this up: owning failure feels like walking into a budget meeting buck-naked under fluorescent lights — every flaw, every fumble, lit up for review. It's vicious. But you know what's worse than screwing up? Trying to gaslight your own team into thinking it didn't happen. They know. They felt the blast. They're still standing in the wreckage, sweeping up the debris.

And when they see you dodge it? That's when the rot sets in — because nothing festers longer than a cover-up. People don't follow perfection. They follow real. They follow the leader who says, "Yeah, I blew it. Here's how we fix it."

And when you do that? You unlock something very powerful: **permission.**

> To try.
> To fail.
> To grow.
> To lead.

You give them the green light to take risks without fear of getting benched. And that's everything.

Why It Matters

Why should you care about any of this when your inbox is a digital dumpster fire and your caffeine's waving the white flag? Because this isn't theory.

It's leadership that knows what it's fighting for. It's the razor-thin line between teams that coast and teams that crush it. Between people who just clock in and people who show the hell up. Between a job and a mission.

So here they are — the six: trust, connection, communication, EQ, culture, and accountability. They're not in this book because they're marketable. They're here because, together, they're bulletproof — naked truths that build, sharpen, and protect.

Master these six and you're no longer managing people — you're magnetizing them. You're building a movement: a living, breathing force that pulls people in and keeps them fighting for something *worth* fighting for.

Think this is overhyped? Let's hit you with the facts.

Gallup — yep, the big dogs — ran the numbers. Only 15 percent of employees are actually engaged at work.

The other 85 percent? They're halfway through a TikTok spiral before you've even finished running the Monday morning huddle.

But here's where it gets loud: teams that are lit up — the ones with real leaders at the helm — don't crawl, they crush. And the numbers back it up: they pull in 147 percent higher earnings per share. Yeah, that's not a typo. Let it marinate for a second.

Translation — leadership matters. **A lot.**

How Revolutions Start

Let me be crystal clear. Leadership isn't a highlight reel for clout-chasing wannabes — it's the grind no one posts about. It's the tone you set before a single word leaves your mouth. The silence you hold when everyone else is slinging BS. It's leading from the marrow out, with conviction so deep people believe before the results even drop.

Because real leadership isn't cosmetic — it's kinetic. You're either breathing life into your people or draining it out of them. There's no safe middle.

When your team knows you've got their backs and they know exactly what you stand for — that's when trust stops being some vague value scrawled on a wall and becomes your brand. It's the way you move. The way the room shifts when you walk in.

And your people? They don't just roll in — they throw down like the mission's personal. Because when you lead with that kind of clarity, it doesn't just change outcomes.

> It changes the culture.
> It changes the team.
> It changes everything.

And the wildest part? Your people start showing up like they helped build the place — because deep down, they know they did. That's when you stop leading a team and start leading a revolution.

The Young Guns Are Here

Today's new wave of leaders? They're not interested in polishing the relics of yesterday's rulebook. They're shredding it and carving new commandments into concrete with zero regard for how it's always been done. This isn't a trendy phase or some company rebrand dressed in softer fonts and a stylish guidebook. It's a full-throttle uprising. Ditch the blazer, the playbook, the pretending. What's replacing it is personal. It's human. It's connected in a way the old-school model couldn't even fake, and it's hitting deeper than any corporate pep rally dressed up as strategy ever could.

And these new leaders? They get it. They're not hoarding power — they're tossing it out like confetti. They're not gatekeeping the mic — they're passing it around. They're not waiting for permission — they're raising the stakes and saying, "Let's go." They've ditched the mask, the script, the illusion of perfection, and given their teams permission to do the same.

They're leading naked — not as a tagline but as truth. Exposed with everything on the line — nothing staged, nothing fake, and nothing left to hide.

They're redefining what strength looks like in a leader.

> Not as dominance but as presence.
> Not as fear but as trust.
> Not as control but as courage.

They own their mistakes — loud and clear. They guard boundaries and treat conflict as a catalyst for growth, not a threat. These aren't your grandfather's executives; they're system breakers, straight-shooters, cultural architects — tearing down what's stale and building something wildly better.

This isn't a phase. This is the future of leadership.

The All-Access Pass

Alright — let's cut the pretense. If you're holding this book, you didn't wander in here by accident. People who buy leadership books aren't bored — they're searching. Pulling. Stretching toward something bigger than their current title, paycheck, or set of expectations.

Maybe you've been wrestling that imposter demon — the one that keeps telling you you're one slip away from being exposed. Cool.

That means you're actually pushing yourself, not sleepwalking. Or maybe you're stuck in that maddening "I'm fine" limbo — functional, competent, even respected... but unfulfilled. That's the slow death no one warns you about. It looks harmless until it rots your ambition from the inside out.

And then there are the rookies — the leaders stepping into the seat for the first time or in front of a new team. You're not off track — you're still figuring out the terrain. You're discovering the weight of authority, the responsibility of a team watching your every move, the pressure to prove yourself before you even understand the rules. But here's the secret: leadership has never been about knowing everything. It's about showing up curious, humble, and brave enough to build trust before you flex authority. The weight of that new title is heavier than it looks — but that's the point. The weight you carry will always shape the lives you lead. Start this right, and everything else will follow.

And of course, there's the crew who'll see themselves in every page — the ones with revolution boiling under their skin. You're not drowning. You're not confused. You're fed up because the room you're in is too small for the vision you keep dragging around. You feel the edges. You feel the containment. You feel the ceiling pretending it's a sky. You're restless because you know you're built for more — and the life you're living keeps asking you to shrink.

Different backgrounds. Different battles. Different reasons for picking up this book — many not even listed. But they all lead to the same truth: ***you're here because you want more.***

More impact. More meaning. More alignment. More influence in your leadership and more courage in the way you show up. You want to say the right thing and mean it. Lead the room and feel like you belong there. Build something worth sacrificing for instead of performing leadership like it's a corporate talent show.

The cost of inaction? Whether you've been pretending, plateauing, finding your footing, or quietly outgrowing your cage, staying where you are leads to the same ending: emptiness. Heavy, silent, suffocatingly empty. And you deserve more than that.

So let's rip off whatever label fits you and get real. This chapter is your all-access pass — not to some starched, PowerPoint-friendly version of leadership, but to the kind that makes people stop mid-sentence because they can feel the authenticity bleeding through. The kind that scares the timid, electrifies the willing, and pulls teams into a mission bigger than themselves.

If you're ready, turn the page.

If you're not?

You will be by the time we're done.

Naked Trust

STRIPPING DOWN TO THE FOUNDATION OF LEADERSHIP

"Trust is the story your people tell when you're not in the room."

MONA VOGELE

Trust, Stripped To The Bone

Trust. It's that mythical thing we're all supposed to have in each other, but let's face it — sometimes it feels about as real as Bigfoot. The reality? It's oxygen. Without it, you're gasping for air, and your team? Flailing harder than a kid in swim class who just realized there's no shallow end.

We've all been spoon-fed the illusion — and too many leaders swallow it whole — that trust comes from a smile plastered on 24/7 or the open-door policy nobody actually walks through.

We confuse it with free bagels in the break room, praising mediocrity to "boost morale," and leaders who promise feedback but deliver it so watered down it couldn't bruise a grape.

We even mistake it for polished town halls, motivational posters, and the relentless drumbeat of "everything's great, keep doing what you're doing."

But none of that earns trust — it just buys silence. It's management from the cheap seats. And when leaders bank on polish and positivity to gain loyalty, they don't get loyalty — they get masks. People will smile back, nod in meetings, keep quiet, and never believe a word you say.

Because trust doesn't give a damn about charisma or bagels or your open-door policy. It's not a perk, it's not a vibe — it's a decision. And it's made by your people moment by moment, based on how you show up when the grind gets hard and the stakes go nuclear.

So here's the deal: we're stripping trust to the bone. Just the facts: why you need it, how to earn it, and what happens when you don't.

The Savage Trinity

Whether it's in boardrooms or break rooms, here's where most people get sloppy: they sling around *trust, credibility, and integrity* like they're the same color of Skittles in a candy bowl. They're related, sure, but they're not triplets. They're the messy, dysfunctional family that makes or breaks your reputation.

Here's the breakdown:

- **Integrity — who you are.**

  It's your moral compass, the spine that keeps you upright when nobody's watching. Screw this up and you're just another slick talker who folds the second temptation whispers in your ear.

  → Do you do what you say?

- **Credibility — how others see you.**

  It's your receipts — the track record, the expertise, the proof you can actually deliver more than hype and a nice "we're in this together" speech. No receipts, no respect.

  → Do I believe what you're saying?

- **Trust — the outcome.**

  It's what you earn once people witness your integrity in action and your credibility stacks up. It's the confidence you show when things get ugly, when it's costly, when it actually matters.

  → Do I believe you've got my back?

Here's what it looks like in the business world:

High integrity but no credibility? That's the wide-eyed intern who'd never steal a stapler, shows up early, and double-checks every rule in the handbook — but can't deliver results, hit deadlines, or even prove they know what they're doing. Solid character, zero track record. You'd trust them with your wallet but not your bottom line.

High credibility but no integrity? That's the rainmaker sales exec who crushes quotas, dazzles in meetings, and always has the data to back them up — but will cut corners, take credit for other people's work, and sell out their team if it means another win. Brilliant track record, rotten spine. You believe their numbers but not their word.

Without credibility and integrity, trust never shows up. But nail both? That's the person whose name carries weight and whose actions hold water. That's when you unlock trust — the kind that fuels loyalty, innovation, and legacies that actually last. So stop tossing these words around like they're synonyms. They're not. They're a savage trinity — and if you're not building all three, you're not leading; you're performing.

Life's plot twist? Even when you've got the trifecta locked in, you're still not safe. I know because I've lived it. I had the receipts and still got burned. What I learned is that trust isn't just earned — it's tested.

From Mascot To Mercenary

Ten years. That's how long I chased the leadership high — like a junkie mainlining promises that evaporated the second reality hit. Branded T-shirt? Wore it like armor. Tattooed logo? Came dangerously close. I wasn't just in the game — I was the poster child for it. And then came the hook — the kind that doesn't just sting but buries deep before you even realize you're bleeding.

I was in — handpicked for the so-called leadership elite. The holy grail of corporate training. I even crushed it so hard they asked me back the next year as a liaison. Me. Guiding the next round of eager believers. One inspirational latte away from sainthood.

Excited? That word doesn't even brush the surface. I thought I was walking into a cheer squad practice — instead, I landed at the library during finals week. My energy didn't inspire — it annoyed.

Was there feedback? Nope, it was MIA. But gossip — that was an all-you-can-eat buffet. The same people who touted "timely feedback" as leadership doctrine suddenly went mute. And the silence wasn't golden — it was spirit-breaking. You know that feeling when the questions creep in?

> Do I belong here?
> Am I the problem?
> Should I just disappear?

Yeah. That.

I didn't just lose faith in *them*. I started losing faith in *me*. But rock bottom's twisted gift? It makes things painfully clear in a way no textbook or workshop ever could. Because when you're flat on your back, you start seeing things differently.

Trust isn't some warm, fuzzy mantra you toss around at company retreats — it's the one true lifeline. Without it, you're the blindfolded fool leading your team straight off a cliff and calling it team-building on the way down.

That savage slap of rejection didn't just wake me up — it ripped the blinders off and shoved my face into the merciless core of leadership. When the course ended, I wanted to Houdini my way out — smoke bomb, trap door, gone. But instead, I stayed. I squared up, choked down my pride, and asked for feedback. And when it came, it hit like a freight train through a concrete wall: "Overzealous. Disruptive."

The very thing I thought was my ace card — my so-called magic wand — was stamped a liability. And the question that won't shut up: why the hell did I have to drag it out of them? Why didn't someone step up, look me in the eye, and say, "You're missing the mark" — in real time, when it actually mattered?

That's not leadership — that's betrayal. The kind that hits like a punch to the solar plexus and leaves you gasping for air. It didn't just sting. It gutted me. But pain has a way of planting something powerful. That was the moment I made a vow: I would become the leader they weren't. Not perfect. Just real.

This experience didn't just tweak how I led; it rewired me from the inside out. Real leaders don't wait for permission to do better. They step up, call out BS, and make damn sure no one has to ask for what should have been given freely.

In a world full of smooth-talking managers, professional grifters, and politicians who'd sell out their grandma for a viral TikTok clip, trust is the only currency that still holds value. Nothing stands without it — not teams, not leaders, not legacies.

→ And when it's missing? You feel it.

Projects crawl slower than airport security lines. Meetings feel like reruns. Decisions? An endless game of tug-of-war. And costs?

They soar when "collaboration" is really just everyone running their own leg of *The Amazing Race* — but no one remembered the map. The question is, will you spot the warning signs before it's too late?

Misalignment In Uniform

Teams that aren't aligned don't just stall — they self-destruct. What starts as a few missed cues turns into crossed wires, clashing egos, and chaos disguised as productivity. Everyone's moving, but no one's moving together. And any hope of progress? Forget it.

Trust is the sync button. Without it, your team is just a sideline circus of mismatched plays, blown coverages, and egos running routes no one called.

Case in Point: The Golden State Warriors

The 2018–2019 Golden State Warriors were the kind of team that made opponents question why they even laced up. Stephen Curry, Kevin Durant, Klay Thompson, Draymond Green — the Avengers in sneakers. On paper, they weren't good — they were terrifying. But paper doesn't show the fractures underneath, and the dynasty had already started to crack.

It all came to a head during a game against the Clippers. The final seconds. Green snatched a rebound and decided to take it coast to coast instead of passing to Durant, who was wide open. The result? Turnover. Overtime loss. Then the fireworks — a sideline blowup so loud it echoed through the league.

Green's credibility took a hit. Durant's silence about his looming free agency fed doubt. The uncertainty ate away at the team's integrity. The trust that once made them unstoppable started to wobble.

The Warriors still dominated most of the season — talent can carry a team that far — but the spark that made them magical was flickering. What had once been telepathic chemistry became tense choreography. Everyone played their part, but the rhythm was off.

Then came the injuries — first Durant, then Klay. Two pillars down, and suddenly the cracks that had been patched over with wins split wide open. The dynasty didn't fall because the skill ran out; it fell because trust did. Talent wins games; trust builds dynasties. You can have a roster full of superstars, but if no one believes the guy next to them will pass the ball when it matters, you're just stat-chasers in matching uniforms.

Coach Kerr tried to hold it together — respect where it's due — but even the best leaders can't out-coach mistrust. That summer, Durant walked. The Warriors' glow dimmed, their dominance disrupted. The kingdom wasn't destroyed, but it was shaken to its core.

Of course, champions evolve. The Warriors would rebuild, adapt, and eventually reclaim their crown in 2022. But this story isn't about redemption — it's about the fracture that forced it.

Your arena might look different, but the truth is the same: when trust falters, collapse isn't a possibility — it's a countdown. So ask yourself: are you protecting trust like your reputation depends on it, or just papering over the cracks your leadership left behind?

The Corporate Battlefield

The boardroom may not have jerseys or stadium lights, but it's still a bare-knuckle brawl. And when trust goes, the fallout is brutal: talent walks, customers bail, and "untouchable" companies hit the floor.

Dieselgate: The High Cost of Deception

Volkswagen's emissions scandal wasn't a stumble — it was a full-throttle crash into the wall of public trust. Not a mistake, but a scheme — a calculated, cold-blooded con. They rigged software to cheat emissions tests, making their "clean diesel" cars look greener than a yoga retreat in Oregon while those engines were spewing toxins like they had a two-pack-a-day habit.

VW's leaders didn't just bend the rules; they ignored them. This wasn't shady — it was sinister. A masquerade ball of deception, and VW showed up in the gaudiest mask. Integrity folded, and the backbone snapped.

For years, they touted "clean diesel" as their crown jewel, stacking up accolades and marketing campaigns as proof. But credibility only holds if the receipts are real. When the lie surfaced, every glossy ad became Exhibit A in the public trial of fraud.

With integrity trashed and credibility exposed as counterfeit, trust evaporated. Customers weren't just disappointed — they were furious. Billions in fines, stock prices in freefall, and a recall tsunami followed. VW thought they were being clever. What they got was a front-row seat to a reputation meltdown.

Trust doesn't take shape in the spotlight — it's forged in the quiet, behind-the-scenes decisions no one notices until the fallout rips through the headlines. Shortcuts might save you time today, but they erode integrity, shred credibility, and nuke trust. And once all three collapse? The climb back is brutal.

Some survive. Most don't. Then there are the few who own their wreckage instead of burying it — leaders who prove that leadership isn't born in the win — it's forged in the rebuild.

Meltdown in the Freezer Aisle

Some brands crack under pressure; others set the bar. Blue Bell Ice Cream? They faced a nightmare that could've melted them into history — and still managed to turn it into a case study in doing the right thing: humanity over profits, people over pints.

Flashback to 2015. Listeria was found in their ice cream. Not rumors. People died. The same brand selling "hometown comfort in a carton" was suddenly a headline nobody wanted on their table. Most companies? They'd lawyer up, dodge cameras, and pump out a soulless "safety is our top priority" statement. Not Blue Bell.

Integrity — front and center. They didn't duck. They didn't minimize. They became the first ice cream company in U.S. history to yank every single pint, bar, and sandwich off the shelves. Nationwide. Trucks recalled mid-route. Factories shut down. Freezers went dark. Millions lost. The message was clear: they put lives ahead of ledgers in a move so bold most legal teams would've called it corporate suicide.

Credibility — proven. While the store shelves sat empty, Blue Bell rebuilt. They tore down processes, scrubbed plants top to bottom, rewired safety protocols, retrained staff, and didn't set foot back on the market until they could show receipts. Their comeback wasn't a press release — it was a slow, deliberate march back into stores, one region at a time, with proof they'd done the hard, ugly work.

Trust — rebuilt. When Blue Bell hit the shelves again, fans rushed back like it never left — not just for ice cream, but for what it represented: a company that torched its own empire rather than gamble with human lives. That loyalty was respect, hardened in crisis.

When trust is on the line, you don't whisper apologies into the void. You don't bury the mess under corporate spin. You burn it all down if you have to. Blue Bell proved that integrity, credibility, and trust aren't soft skills — they're the only capital that still holds value when everything else goes cold.

A Modern Epidemic

These aren't just war stories swapped over conference room coffee. They're undeniable proof that trust decides everything: who rises, who rots, who gets remembered, and who gets buried.

This isn't a glitch in the system. It's an epidemic, and the numbers are unforgiving. According to the Edelman Trust Barometer, 82 percent of employees don't believe their boss tells them the truth.

Let that rattle around your brain for a second. That's not just a footnote — it's a siren. Leaders need to take this seriously. When you dodge brutal realities or spin the facts, trust doesn't quietly leave the room — it evaporates like tequila at a frat party.

 **You want a crew that moves mountains?** Then protect integrity, guard credibility, and build trust. Daily.

Ignore this savage trinity and watch your team splinter into cliques, turf wars, and backstage brawls for status and control.

When It Pays Dividends

Trust is a force multiplier — it amplifies everything. When it's high, teams move faster, stress less, and work like they've got a live wire running through their veins. Deadlines don't drag. Projects don't stall. Communication flows. Budgets stay tight. People stay focused. And drama? It doesn't even show up to the party.

Bottom line? Trust is the ROI no one bothers to track — until it's gone. Still need proof? Patagonia built an empire on it.

Surf's Up Boss

If trust were a brand, Patagonia would be the poster child. This isn't just a company with a good reputation. It's a mission-driven machine that's turned trust into its operating system — *and* its superpower. The company's founder didn't just sprinkle it into the handbook — he built a culture where trust gave people the freedom to run, not wait for permission.

→ Micromanagement? Out.
→ Rigid hierarchy? Not even close.

Point proven: the now-iconic "Let My People Go Surfing" policy —
and yeah, it's exactly what it sounds like. When the surf's up,
employees can drop everything, grab their board, and hit the
waves. No permission slips. No side-eyes. No guilt trips.

Looks like a perk, doesn't it? Nope. It's a middle finger to toxic
workplace norms. It screams, "We believe you can dominate at
work — and still have a life outside of it."

And what happened? They didn't just get results — they sparked
a movement. Employee engagement didn't just climb — it went
orbital. Turnover? Practically vanished. Patagonia didn't stay a
brand — it transformed into a belief system, with loyalty so die-
hard it makes religion look like a weekend hobby.

Stripped down: earning trust is not some HR-flavored hug-it-out
concept. It's what unleashes passion, fuels loyalty, and keeps
your people charging through recessions, reinventions, and every
curveball in between. This wasn't a strategy. They made trust
their identity. And the payoff? A brand people don't just work for
or buy from — they believe in.

For Patagonia, it was never *if* trust mattered — it was how far
they'd go to earn it. Today, they're catching waves while others
are still wading in. The question now? How do you start building
yours?

The Trust Gauntlet

By now, you get it — trust isn't a "nice-to-have." You can't Amazon
Prime it, two-day ship it, or fake-it-'til-you-make-it. It's more
like planting seeds than downloading an app. It takes time,

intention, and the guts to show up consistently — even when it's inconvenient. Here's the framework, starting with transparency.

Transparency on Repeat: The Power Play

Transparency isn't some "let's hold hands and share our feelings" nonsense — it's slamming the hard facts on the table before anyone asks. It's the move that says: "I've got nothing to hide — zoom in if you want." Own the wins. Own the losses.

Because trust doesn't grow in the dark. It thrives in the light — fed by honesty, forged in consistency.

The thing is (and everyone knows it), the truth always surfaces. And when it does, it better be on your terms. But don't think one big show of honesty will cut it. It won't. If you shine the light once and then vanish into the shadows, people won't remember the spotlight — they'll remember the blackout.

Transparency only works if you keep showing up.

> Every follow-through.
> Every kept promise.
> Every day.

Drop the ball, and doubt kicks in. And doubt? That sneaky little bastard multiplies fast. Once it's in, it spreads — whispers turn into rumors, side-eyes replace confidence, and suddenly you're not leading a team — you're refereeing suspicion.

Talk is cheap. Proof is the real currency. Be the kind of reliable that makes gravity look optional. Because when it counts, people don't follow titles. They follow trust — built on transparency, reinforced by consistency, and delivered without excuses.

Stop. Listen. Build.

Your team's talking. The question is, are you hearing them — or just polishing your next smart-sounding line? Listening isn't nodding like a dashboard bobblehead. It's locking in — words, subtext, silences, the whole frequency. That's where trust takes root. That's where monologues die and dialogue kicks in. When people know their voice isn't noise, everything shifts. Roadblocks crack. Conviction gets louder. Momentum starts to move in ways you can't fake or force.

Think I'm exaggerating? Look at Weight Watchers (now WW). When Mindy Grossman took the helm of WW, she didn't arrive with the usual "sit down, shut up, let me fix you" routine. She came in, tuned in, and started listening — from the boardroom to the mailroom. Like a DJ spinning the perfect set, she caught the rhythm of the company through its people.

→   The result? A real-world blueprint for listening.

By giving everyone a seat at the table — from C-suite execs to interns — she ignited creativity and collaboration. The brand that once felt dated and diet-obsessed became a wellness brand — bolder, modern, alive. WW didn't just survive — it reinvented itself.

 **You want results like that?** Turn up the volume on your team's voices. Listening isn't passive — it's how you catch signals, read the energy, and spot what's said and unsaid. It's creativity on blast, innovation unchained, and collaboration in overdrive.

So stop filling the air with your own voice. Start tuning in. Let listening do the heavy lifting — and watch what your team builds when they know they've actually been heard.

The Courage to Unclench

Here's where most leaders get sweaty palms: trust falls. And not the cheesy company off-site kind where you hope Bob from accounting doesn't drop you. The real kind. Vulnerability. Showing up with all your flaws, admitting you're not perfect, and letting people see the human behind the title. It's not weakness — it's the moment "the boss" becomes a leader worth following.

Pat Lencioni calls it "vulnerability trust." Owning your humanity, warts and all, and betting your team won't just catch you — they'll rise with you. That's the trust fall — but it's only the start.

The free fall? That's leadership with no parachute — stepping off the edge with nothing but guts and conviction, daring your people to prove you were right to bet on them.

It's the moment you hand over the reins, let them trip, bruise, and rise — because you're *all-in* on their ascent. That's not weakness. That's savage-level faith — equal parts courage and chaos, and the only kind that builds legends.

Perfect example: Bob Chapman, CEO of Barry-Wehmiller, asked the one question most leaders are too scared to even whisper: "What if I just... let my people lead?"

Cute on a coffee mug, sure. Except Chapman actually did it. No micromanaging. No helicopter hovering. He unclenched — hard. He handed over real decisions with real consequences and let his people own every glorious, terrifying outcome.

- → Risky? You better believe it.
- → Necessary? Absolutely.
- → The result? Damn near mythic.

His *Truly Human Leadership* didn't just boost morale — it blew the lid off. People stopped just doing their jobs and started showing up like the mission had their name on it. Confidence surged. Creativity soared. Loyalty locked in like muscle memory.

Trusting your team doesn't mean disappearing — it means you stop being the ceiling on their potential. That's how you build leaders, not sheep. And here's the kicker: this isn't a new concept — it's the oldest cheat code in leadership.

The tragedy? Most leaders are too busy white-knuckling control to ever use it.

The Unshakable Foundation

Every leader worth their weight in black coffee knows this: trust is the foundation of every successful team, project, and organization. Without it, the whole structure buckles.

It's no secret — buildings don't just topple out of nowhere. They give way because of cracks left ignored. Same with teams. It's rarely the headline crisis that breaks an organization — it's the fractures leaders overlook until everything caves in on their watch.

But let's be honest — nobody nails it every time. We all screw up: drop the ball, miss the mark, maybe even commit the ultimate workplace sin — running out of coffee before a Monday meeting (a betrayal of biblical proportions). But mistakes aren't fatal. Denial is. That's why you've got to triage. Trust is a living structure that will splinter under pressure unless you've got the guts to face it, fix it, and fortify it.

Here's how you triage when the cracks start to show:

Own It (Fast)
Don't let the rumor mill co-opt the narrative. Call the break before it calls you out. Admit it. Say it straight — even if it stings. Because ignoring the elephant in the room doesn't make it vanish; it just guarantees broken furniture. The fastest way to rebuild? Tell the truth.

Show the Fix
Words are wallpaper — they just cover cracks. You want trust back? Drop the slogans and roll out the paper trail. Hammer in the fix so hard it reverberates. Then do it again. And again. Until doubt has nowhere left to live.

Go Glass-Box Mode
When trust cracks, secrecy speeds the collapse. Drag it into the light. Share the real stuff — the awkward, the messy, the "we're still figuring this out" moments. Short-term discomfort beats long-term doubt. Be radically transparent. Every time.

Prove It on Repeat
Rebuilding trust isn't a one-time stunt — it's a daily grind. Every aligned action is a deposit; every contradiction is a withdrawal. No balance, no trust. Consistency is the currency, and if you're not paying daily, you'll go broke.

Once you've built trust, the real work begins. Protect it like the lifeline it is. Every choice, every word, every silence — either it strengthens the foundation or it starts the next crack. So raise the bar high enough that shortcuts can't reach it, and gossip dies before it grows teeth. Make it so solid that nothing breaks through — every hit ricochets and goes hunting for easier prey.

Because trust won't protect itself — that's your job. And the only fatal move is pretending the gates will hold without you.

Trust In Your Leadership

So, what now? Show up — flawed, fierce, and all in. Listen with the hunger of someone chasing truth — because every pause is holding out a clue. And when the pressure hits — and it will — don't look away. The stumbles, the screw-ups, the "oh crap" moments? They're proof you're in the arena, taking the hits and swinging anyway — doing the hard, glorious, human work of leadership.

Trust isn't built in the comfort of a cushy corner office. It's etched in the daily grind. Get it right and the ripple won't just touch your team — it'll echo into the future. And that future? It isn't going to write itself. Because your story — the one that actually matters — starts now. Make it unforgettable.

Trust me — you've got this. (Pun absolutely intended.)

Naked Bonds

THE STRENGTH OF REAL CONNECTIONS

"Build connections that hit like a power chord—because when people feel it, they won't just follow—they'll amplify your legacy."

MONA VOGELE

Lead Like An Anthem

Ever had a moment of connection hit so hard it feels like a revelation? It shows up unannounced, right in the middle of your life, and everything shifts. Suddenly, it's like you've stepped into a Scorsese scene—time drags, everything slows. Goosebumps rise. The air sharpens. Every instinct says, "Pay attention." That's not some surface-level acquaintance—that's raw, no-filter impact.

And when leadership connects like that? It doesn't just land—it brands itself into your bones. It hits you like the first note of a song that dares you not to feel it.

It demands presence. Unity. A rhythm that screams, "We're doing this. Together."

I know because I grew up in its wake. The rhythm of the '60s didn't chase likes—it tore the sky open. Dylan's lyrics cut like sermons—folk songs turned protest anthems that rattled governments. Joplin poured gasoline on every stage she touched, her voice a howl that cracked the "good girl" mold wide open. Aretha, the Queen of Soul, turned *Respect* into a movement— civil rights, human rights—a generation's demand. And Hendrix? He lit up Woodstock, ripping the national anthem into a battle cry in front of half a million souls.

These weren't just artists—they were architects of something so primal it felt hardwired into your DNA. The ache for belonging. The hunger for change. They were influencers of a generation. They connected through sound the way leaders are meant to influence and connect—through raw realness and unfiltered truth.

Leaders today need to ditch the talking-head zombie act on Zoom and become the anthem that rattles their team's ribcage long after the call drops. You're not managing tasks — you're dropping the track that makes fear irrelevant and momentum inevitable. It's never been about being heard — it's about being felt.

So, forget the podium. Tear down the imaginary stage. Get in the pit and build harmony where the chaos lives. Because that's where connection gets real. Heartbeats sync. Belonging comes alive.

And if you're not willing to drop the beat and meet your people where they actually are? You're not leading — you're breaking the very rhythm you were meant to protect.

The Bassline of Belonging

People aren't just wired for connection — we crave it like oxygen. Always have. From cavemen trading survival hacks over firelight to your Gen Z squad syncing Spotify playlists like emotional Morse code, that instinctive hunger hasn't changed.

> See me.
> Hear me.
> Get me.
> Stand by me.

That's not found in a corner office or in your ability to dominate an investor call with Q3 projections. It's found in connection — the electricity in the room. It's why people don't just go through the motions; they fight for the mission and bet the house on it. Because what matters isn't the words you speak in a meeting —

it's what lands, what lingers, what makes your people whisper, "Oh yeah, I'm in."

Leadership at its core? Influence — made unforgettable through emotional resonance. It hits like a lyric that's been living in your chest, waiting for someone to sing it out loud. It's visceral sonar — pinging straight to the soul, no translation required.

The blunt reality? No one gives a crap about your perfectly crafted mission statement if they feel invisible in the room. You can frame your values, slap them on swag, blast them in all-company emails — but if your people don't feel seen, it's paint over cracks. And cracks don't stay hidden; they spread until the whole foundation caves.

To get loyalty from a crew that shows up like co-founders, not cogs, start seeing them. No roles. No performative posturing. Just humans — flawed, brilliant, burned out, fired up — standing together, linked by grit, carving meaning out of the day-to-day hustle.

And no — I'm not talking about the "we're all family here" propaganda. That's a red flag wrapped in forced fun. Spare us. Most folks are still in therapy from actual family dinners.

What they need isn't artificial unity. They need connection — the unscripted, flesh-and-bone kind. Their quirks. Their beliefs. What makes them laugh. What keeps them grounded. What fuels their drive. Because when people feel seen — not as roles, not as resources, but as real — they come alive.

The psychology of connection is primal. It's baked into our nervous system, hard-wired like the need for air, water, and tacos on a Friday night. Ignore it and your team starts short-circuiting.

> Disengaged.
> Disconnected.
> Disappearing.

Want them to show up like their soul's on the payroll? Then wake up. Loyalty doesn't come from a bonus structure — or your 11th "thoughts and prayers" email blast. It comes from one thing: leadership that feels human.

Leadership that shows up, checks in, and actually sees them — I mean really sees them. The leader who doesn't just say, "Nice work," but knows what it cost. Who doesn't just celebrate the win but respects the work that got it there. That's who they'll follow. Not the spreadsheet wizard or policy parrot. The leader who earns loyalty daily.

So, plug in — or get replaced by someone who will. And if it's the latter, your people won't even blink — they'll already be gone, following the first pulse that actually saw them.

But pull it off and you don't just raise morale — you trigger a full-blown transformation. Not workers, but warriors. Collaborators who build worlds out of whiteboard scribbles. People who throw themselves into the work with everything on the line — no vanity, just flow. And when that happens, the result isn't a metric; it's a movement.

- → Output? Unlocked.
- → Ideas? Unbridled.
- → Innovation? Unrestrained.

That's when leadership stops being tactical and starts becoming transcendent. And when it hits? It disarms cynics and rallies the skeptics. It pulls strangers into orbit and makes them family by choice, not by force. It takes ordinary rooms and turns them into war councils. It's the most untamed, influential power in leadership.

Strip away the corporate-speak, kill the hype, and what's left? A bassline that grabs your people by the spine and whispers:

"You belong. Right here. Right now."

Sounds powerful, right?

The catch? You're leading in a world designed to drown it out.

Leadership Is A Deep Drill

On a regular day? Modern leadership feels like a firehose to the face while someone yells, "Hydrate!" Algorithms mutate daily, hiring pipelines short-circuit like bad wiring, and burnout gets passed around the office like stale donuts — sad and morale-crushing.

Most leaders? They drown in that mess. They skim the surface, confuse motion with progress, and mistake their echo chamber for strategy.

The great ones? They don't chase surface distractions. They cut through the noise, tune in, and lock onto the signal.

The job isn't about doing more — it's about becoming more.

> More grounded.
> More real.
> More human.

The kind of leader who walks in, and the whole room recalibrates. Minds focus. Hearts unlock. The noise dies. And suddenly, the energy feels magnetic, undeniable, inescapable — pulling everyone toward building something incredible.

These leaders know greatness doesn't live on the surface. That's where pretenders skim — clinging to tired rituals like they're hoarding dial-up wisdom from 1997, complete with "you've got mail" vibes. It's safe, sure — but it never reaches people where it matters.

Humans have wrestled with this reckoning for centuries: the pull between surface comfort or deeper greatness. One story that rips the point wide open comes from the fields of Southeast Texas in the early 1900s — dry wind, busted crops, farmers nursing dead soil and broken hopes.

Rumors spread that just beneath their tired boots lay an ocean of potential — crude, power, possibility. But nobody was willing to do the hard work of digging to find out. Surface-level felt safer. Everyone waited for proof instead of building a damn rig.

Enter one oilman with more instinct than evidence and a farmer so desperate the only words left were, "What the hell, let's drill."

At 1,139 feet — BOOM. A full-blown explosion of crude oil, rock, and sky-high potential.

- → The date? January 10, 1901.
- → The gusher? Spindletop.
- → The impact? Game-changing.

It was an eruption that rewrote the future. Overnight, that farmer went from barely scraping by to headline-making rich.

Or did he?

The irony? That farmer was standing on that wealth all along. Oil, power, the future — was right under his boots, waiting. But he never swung the pick. Never struck the ground. Never dug for himself.

The irony in leadership is the same. You're standing on greatness buried just below the surface of your people — chanting "potential" and "possibility" while the real work, the digging, never starts.

Great leaders go subterranean. They get dirty. They get dangerous. They dig — through fear, through doubt, through ego, through the fossilized crust of "this is how we've always done it." They pound until the ground cracks and their team's brilliance blasts to the surface — the kind of brilliance that never shows itself to the casual. It hides, daring only the relentless to drag it out.

The rest? They skim. They polish the obvious. They babysit mediocrity. And they die broke in the Lone Wolf graveyard — circling dirt, kicking up dust, talking tough while sitting on riches they'll never have the guts to claim.

The Power Of The Pack

Let's ditch the "lone wolf" fantasy once and for all. Hollywood loves it — one grim renegade storming through fire in slow motion, cape snapping in the wind like he's Batman moonlighting as a CEO. Looks badass on a movie poster. But in reality? That guy's toast.

The truth is, lone wolf leaders burn out fast. No map, no backup, no fresh perspective. Their people eventually stop following —

not out of rebellion but because no one wants to hitch their future to a martyr with a hero complex. And nobody hands out medals for running yourself ragged; they just stop giving you a seat at the table.

The leaders who last — the ones who build something seismic — don't perch on pedestals. They plant their boots inside the pack, amplifying the grind, unlocking horsepower no one can summon alone. And when a pack surges, it rewrites limits and crushes obstacles that flatten solo stragglers.

Smart leaders torch the hubris, trade distance for proximity, and dig until the pressure erupts. And when it blows? It's not a trickle — it's Spindletop reborn. Not leadership by domination. Leadership by detonation.

So forget the lone-wolf legend. The future belongs to packs bold enough to move as one — teeth bared, eyes forward, claw marks gouged into history — proof that titles mean nothing without the hands that cranked the rig shoulder to shoulder until the earth split and the story rewrote itself.

The Silent Assassin

When you brush off real connection as some kumbaya crap, you're not saving time — you're mortgaging your culture for short-term comfort. And once the culture tanks? You don't just lose momentum.

> You lose respect.
> You lose loyalty.
> You lose influence.

Wondering why your high performers are bailing? Why your all-star team feels like a hostage situation with a 401(k)? It's not the workload. It's you — treating connection like it's optional. You worship KPIs and dashboards while the only metric that moves mountains — people who give a damn — bleeds out in plain sight.

Here's how the unravel starts:

Silos form

If you're not building bridges, you're building bunkers — where collaboration dies. And every wall you ignore turns into a silo faster than you can say "cross-functional."

Resentment simmers

Unseen. Unheard. Undervalued. Your team isn't grumbling anymore — they're plotting their exit strategies between passive-aggressive emails.

Innovation flatlines

No connection? You're not creating the future — you're embalming the past. Burnout isn't coming; it's already sitting at your desk, wearing your logo like a choke chain.

Sound familiar? Yeah, thought so.

Skipping connection isn't a strategy; it's sabotage in a pantsuit. It's leadership malpractice dressed up in performance metrics and a title that doesn't mean crap anymore. You didn't just miss a soft skill — you pulled the pin and walked away. What follows isn't a misunderstanding or a morale dip. It's fallout.

Culture fractures. Energy drains. What used to feel electric now feels transactional and heavy. And when the dust finally settles, the question won't be *why did they leave*. It'll be how did we miss it?

This isn't just a breakdown of trust — it's a controlled demolition of potential.

And the name on the toe tag? *Yours.*

The Fallout

- **Productivity? Meet Quiet Quitting:**
  Think exhaustion is killing your output? Disconnection hits harder. It doesn't just slow progress — it rots it from the inside out. Then you're left babysitting empty suits who show up for the paycheck and bail the second the Wi-Fi hiccups.

  - → Meetings? Background noise.
  - → Deadlines? Sloppy.
  - → The work? Meaningless.

  This isn't hustle. It's hospice.

- **Burnout Becomes a Lifestyle:**
  They're not tired — they're done. Sick days become escape routes. Cameras off, minds shut down, effort on autopilot. This isn't physical fatigue. It's emotional foreclosure. They're not "sick." They've stopped caring.

  - → Avoiding work? No, they're avoiding you.

- **Turnover Town — Population: YOU:**
  No connection means no loyalty. Your office becomes a revolving door, with people coming and going like happy hour at a dive bar. And the ones that stay? They're not your future — they just haven't found an exit plan yet.

  - → The MVPs? Gone. Or disengaged while still on the payroll.

And here's the part they don't print in leadership manuals: this isn't about apathy — it's the aftermath of bad leadership. The result? You didn't just lose a team. You lost everything that could've been.

Collapse or Conquer

Disconnection isn't a hiccup. It's a demolition crew in slow motion — and it doesn't need permission to destroy. It sneaks in — quiet, unassuming — until your high performers go mute. Until the culture, once electric, starts pulsing with doubt and distrust. You don't notice the shift in real time — it's not a fire alarm. It's carbon monoxide, filling the room while everyone pretends to breathe normally. What used to be momentum becomes molasses — every meeting heavier, every decision slower, every spark harder to find.

And then? It drops. No warning — just collapse. Trust splinters. Morale caves. Innovation suffocates in the silence. By the time it hits the company dashboard, it's already too late. What's left is a ghost crew wearing company swag like camouflage — clocking in for paychecks, clocking out on everything else.

This isn't just a problem. It's a full-blown cardiac arrest. You either connect — or you collapse. Full stop. No rescue. Just rubble. And rubble doesn't rebuild itself — you either dig out or get buried.

Feeling queasy yet? Good. That's awareness finally waking you up. Don't sedate it. Don't spin it. Let it burn. Because disconnection isn't fatal — it's fixable.

But not with swag bags, casual Fridays, or a "culture reset" campaign. You can't bribe belonging or PR your way through the wake of disconnection. Real repair takes guts — owning what's broken, having the hard conversations, and rebuilding trust.

Connection that sticks comes when leaders quit outsourcing the work, stare down the mess in the mirror, and own every crack they helped create with unyielding, intentional effort — daily.

The Underground Guide To Loyalty

How do you avoid becoming *that* leader? You know, the one with a team that's one bad Monday away from a collective resignation letter. You connect.

Beyond Job Titles: Meeting the Humans You Lead

If all you see are roles on an org chart, you've already lost. That "marketing guy"? He's a single dad, weekend soccer coach, and the reigning king of guac. Know *that guy*. See the person, not the title, and suddenly they're not following orders — they're following *you*. And nothing can shake that.

Lead with Vulnerability. Drop the "Perfect" Act

Forget perfection. You don't build connection by flexing your flawless streak — you build it by admitting what scares the crap out of you. You want influence? Be real. Real builds bridges faster than bravado ever will. Vulnerability doesn't make you weak — it makes you relatable.

Create Spaces for Real Conversation

Grab a coffee, take a walk, lean against the wall, and just talk. That's where connection grows. Want loyalty? Don't jam it into whatever calendar you pledge allegiance to. Earn it in the unscripted moments where people realize you're not an executive mannequin — you're real, and you're listening.

Confetti for the Underdogs — Why Small Wins Matter

Yeah, the big wins get the headlines. But the small ones? They build belief. That intern who saved the client call? The quiet dev guy who stayed late to fix the glitch no one saw? Confetti them. Loudly. Often. That's how you turn teams into tribes.

Invest in Face Time — On Screen or In Person.

Presence beats proximity. Don't hide behind your inbox like a scared executive cliché. A five-minute video check-in carries more weight than 500 words in a company-wide email. When they see you show up, they'll start showing up for you.

Stop Fixing — Start Feeling

People can smell counterfeit compassion a mile away. They know when you're nodding along while mentally drafting your reply. So stop. Feel the weight they're carrying. See it from their side without rushing to duct-tape a solution.

The Proving Ground

Connection isn't a side hustle — it's your oxygen. Without it, your business isn't alive; it's on life support. Ignore your team, and they'll yank the IV before walking out the door. And exit interviews? Just autopsies you should've seen coming.

You don't need warm bodies filling seats — you need hell-yes humans fighting for the mission because they've chosen it, and you. This isn't fantasy; it's the proving ground. The place where leaders are forged into steel — or shattered into dust. The place between what you say and what you deliver. Every broken promise is a crack in your armor; every hollow word is another piece of shrapnel. The pressure's closing in — no shields, no respawns. You either choke or you lead. This is leadership in the trenches.

- → The stakes? Real.
- → The clock? Ruthless.
- → The cavalry? Forget it — you *are* the cavalry.

Still skeptical? Let me show you what it looks like when connection is the last thread holding everything together — and the rope you climb back up on.

The Reckoning: Ford's Human Comeback

It was the mid-2000s. Ford wasn't just limping — it was a Mustang on blocks, paint fading, and the glory days looking like a rearview mirror fantasy. Departments were at war. Innovation slammed into reverse. Cash was hemorrhaging faster than a busted radiator. Hope wasn't just thin — it was vanishing, traded in for survival mode and denial. And nothing could stop the gasping sound of a company suffocating on its own fumes.

Competitors were leaving Ford choking on their exhaust while the company bickered over who had the keys. The brand once synonymous with American ingenuity was failing — drowning in silos, pride, and bureaucratic red tape. Its engine sputtered as the giant that once ruled the road was running out of gas, and no one inside could deny it.

Then came the play that changed everything. It was 2006. In walked Alan Mulally — not just another suit, but a straight shooter with steel in his voice. Rumor has it, he lobbed the first grenade across the bow with, "What are we doing that's stupid?" Whether that's true or not, it wasn't far off. He challenged employees to face what was broken and stop pretending it wasn't. And it wasn't just a challenge — it was a sledgehammer through the corporate façade. For the first time in years, people stopped posturing and started listening. From there, he went to work — rebuilding the giant with a call to arms:

> *One Ford. One mission. One team.*

Gone was the old-school, top-down, lone-wolf leadership. He didn't command from a throne. He connected. And he rewrote the playbook by doing what most leaders are too afraid to do — he made it human.

The Five Moves That Saved Ford

 **Radical Transparency**
Mulally's weekly reviews weren't meetings — they were firing lines. Leaders had to color-code their updates: green, yellow, or red. Nobody dared show red — until someone did. The room braced for impact.

What did Mulally do? He clapped. Not sarcastically — sincerely. He celebrated the honesty and turned it into momentum. That wasn't just a meeting — it was a cultural earthquake.

 **Silo Smashing**
Before Mulally, Ford's departments were medieval fiefdoms — swords drawn, backs turned. He crushed that fast. "One Ford" wasn't a slogan — it was a ceasefire. Collaboration replaced turf wars. Teams shared knowledge. And before they knew it, the beast started humming again.

 ### Personal Connection

This guy wasn't hiding behind bulletproof glass. He was on the floor — learning names, remembering birthdays, asking about kids. "Everyone matters" wasn't a tagline — it was the rhythm he walked to. And when people felt seen, they stopped phoning it in and began to fight like hell for the mission.

Humility Meets Optimism

Even while the house burned, Mulally didn't blink. No finger-pointing. No tantrums. Just measured, surgical calm. He didn't sugarcoat the crisis, but he never let it own the room. That kind of resolve didn't just anchor the team — it spread through them. Panic died. Focus took hold.

A Simple North Star

Most companies drown in vanity metrics. Mulally gave Ford three: quality, safety, and efficiency. That's it. If a decision didn't serve those, it didn't happen. No more chasing shiny objects. Just a laser-beam focus that cut through decades of sludge and gave the company its momentum back.

He didn't need a miracle — he gave them something to believe in, and the conviction to back it up. That was the strategy: connection. And it didn't just save Ford — it rewired the company's DNA, proving that when leaders choose people over posturing, they don't just build products — they build empires.

The Ford Rebellion

Mulally didn't just steer Ford out of the grave — they came back swinging. While other automakers in 2008 lined up like panhandlers for government bailouts, Ford held the line. No handouts. No surrender. Just resolve, determination, and a huge firestorm of momentum.

→ Stock? Skyrocketed.
→ Morale? Reborn.
→ Teams? Locked in and lethal.

And the reason wasn't shinier cars, louder ads, or blind luck. Mulally didn't lead with fear or flex titles — he led with trust, and trust built connection. He handed people honesty, accountability, and a seat at the table — and they paid him back with everything they had. That's the blueprint for leaders everywhere.

Lead by earning trust — not demanding it.
Lead by unleashing potential — not burying it.
Lead with influence that's earned — not fear you force.

The most formidable leader in the room isn't the one who controls everything — it's the one who unleashes the brilliance in their people to build something unstoppable. And Ford proved it. Connection was the paper-thin line between collapse and comeback.

This isn't just a case study you quote in the company newsletter. It's a hard stop to the stagnant idea that people are secondary to performance. Mulally knew this above all else: connection doesn't just strengthen leverage — it is the leverage.

That's what naked leadership does:

It moves people.
It inspires action.
It builds belief.
It rewrites the future.

No Illusions — Only Impact

Leadership is full of glorious human complexity. Titles mean nothing. Dashboards mean less. The only thing that counts is energy that moves people — that gravitational pull that makes them feel something, believe something, and rise because of it.

→ Without connection? You're just noise.

→ With it? You become the signal.

So lead like Mulally — human first. It's time to bury the lone-wolf mentality and harness the power of the pack. Don't chase quick wins. Don't settle for hollow victories. Don't confuse motion with momentum. Trade illusion for impact and reshape the way you show up — for your team, your mission, and yourself.

REMEMBER

Leadership isn't a solo act — it's a relay. Your energy doesn't end with you; it passes through the team, gathering force with every handoff. Lone wolves burn out. Packs take ground, mile after mile, because they refuse to run alone.

Look around. Your people aren't waiting for another "company vision" slideshow. They're waiting for you. Not the curated version. **You.** The one brave enough to look them in the eye and not blink. To ask the hard questions. To see them — and let yourself be seen.

So walk the floor.
Start the conversation.
Send the text.
Stand in the discomfort.

Because when the walls begin to close in, only connection — born out of earned trust — holds the line. Be the leader who isn't just lip service but marrow-deep in the fight.

Your team? They're ready to rise.

The question is — are you the one they'll rise for?

Naked Communication

THE BATTLEFIELD RADIO OF LEADERSHIP

"Communication isn't a skill; it's survival instinct wrapped in courage."

MONA VOGELE

Welcome To The Jungle Of Verbal Warfare

Let's not pretend. Communication isn't some neat little art form. It can be a full-blown war zone, where every "quick chat" is a potential ambush, every "just circling back" email a potential hand grenade with a smiley face.

One misread text, one half-baked reply, one tone-deaf call, and boom—you've abandoned a teammate, nuked a deadline, or sparked an office-wide emoji standoff.

We've all been in the meeting where the boss reads silence as "understood" while the team's blinking in Morse code for help. It's like juggling flaming chainsaws blindfolded—praying you don't decapitate your reputation or torch your entire team dynamic.

So yeah—welcome to the jungle, baby. No compass. No decoder ring. Just overcomplication wrapped in politeness and misfires. But good news—we're about to machete our way through this jungle, gut the meaningless nods, and slash the unfiltered back-and-forth down to its bare bones. No more pretending to understand when every fiber of your being is screaming "WTH!"

This isn't communication as you've been sold it. This is feral, unarmored, and dangerous enough to burn the whole façade down. Ready or not, this is reveille—fall in.

Military Bravado And Family Dinners

No, I wasn't military. But you wouldn't know it if you sat down at our dinner table. My childhood was scored by war stories, passed like mashed potatoes between my grandfather, dad, and brothers. These weren't Hollywood hero edits with soaring soundtracks. They were real accounts of survival — grit in the teeth and blood in the bootlaces. Forget corporate icebreakers — this was dinner conversation plated with struggle, washed down with life-or-death.

And if you had the guts to listen — somewhere between bites of Mom's meatloaf — you'd hear it. Beneath the courage, camo, and the dark-as-night humor was something bigger: a pulse. The untamed beat of what leadership sounds like when it's stripped to survival.

The story that still haunts my bones? Bat 21. Not just a story about making it out alive, but straight-up elite training in communication under pressure. A make-or-break reminder that hits like a shot of cold adrenaline — because saying the right thing at the right moment is the high-stakes difference between rescue and ruin.

Different battlefield. Same stakes. Every leader faces that no-room-for-error moment. What you say in that instant decides whether you leave leading — or limping.

The Man Who Outplayed Death

The missile didn't just strike — it stalked. It chased that aircraft like it had unfinished business, a personal vendetta with destruction written into its circuitry. One second, he was a 53-year-old Air Force officer in control. The next, he was a man tumbling through the sky as his plane exploded into a fireball behind him. Thousands of pieces. Five crew members — gone in an instant. He was the only one left.

Call Sign: Bat 21 Bravo.
Real Name: Lt. Col. Iceal "Gene" Hambleton.

His parachute snapped open like a slap to the heavens, the clouds below masking the nightmare underneath. But war's carnage wasn't new — it was etched into the muscle memory of every breath.

It was April 2, 1972. Easter Sunday. But there was no resurrection waiting for him on the ground — only war. The jungle didn't greet him; it consumed him. And what lay ahead wasn't survival — it was the test of everything he was.

As night draped its heavy cloak over South Vietnam, the man who'd survived the explosion found himself alone and surrounded by the fury of one of the largest enemy offensives of the Vietnam War.

At first light, U.S. forces had his location down to within thirty feet — yes, thirty — and a wall of enemy artillery. An immediate rescue attempt was launched, but the jungle answered first.

The first bird to fall was Blueghost 39, a Huey ripped from the sky by a wall of ground fire. It was clear, rescue wasn't impossible. It was suicidal. So they lit up the sky instead.

For days, a relentless pounding followed — U.S. forces hammering North Vietnamese gun positions around Hambleton's location with everything they had. Bombs. Strafing runs. Jets screamed overhead like wrath incarnate. American pilots flew through hell without blinking — warbirds slicing the sky into ribbons, keeping the enemy at bay.

April 6. Dawn cracked open, and the order came again — another rescue attempt on the table. The 37th Air Rescue and

Recovery Squadron — based in Da Nang and wired for impossible missions — lifted off to do what they did best: punch through the inferno, grab Bat 21, muscle back out, and live to tell the tale.

But the enemy had other plans. As the mission unfolded that morning, Hambleton watched from the ground as the lead helicopter took savage ground fire — rounds tearing through its hull like a buzzsaw through sheet metal — but the crew held on. They wanted another run. They wanted him. Instead, they were forced to turn back, barely making it to safety in one piece.

Later that day, more helicopters punched back into the fire. My brother Mike was on one of them — twenty-one years old, a U.S. Air Force Pararescueman strapped into a bird with other gunners and medics who lived on the edge, men wired with a kind of courage most people never even glimpse in themselves.

But this was no rescue mission — it was a thunder run into death's backyard.

As they closed in on Hambleton's position, hope hung in the air for a split second — then the jungle roared to life. Anti-aircraft guns and automatic weapons turned the canopy into a kill box. One of the birds, Jolly Green 67, took hit after hit before spiraling downward and crashing in flames.

Hambleton saw it fall — helpless — this time near his position. Six souls lost, right in front of him.

Years later, reflecting on the rescue, Hambleton said watching six men die while trying to save him was "a hell of a price to pay for one life." Words that still carry weight today.

But these men? They're stitched together by a creed branded in bone, carved deeper than fear:

"That Others May Live."

Surrender didn't exist in their world. My brother. The pilots. The other gunners and medics. These weren't just airmen — they were zealots of a creed that outlawed retreat. They strapped in knowing damn well they might not come back — because leaving a man behind? That's never an option.

That's when a new plan emerged — one as bold as it was desperate. If they couldn't get to Hambleton, he'd have to get to them.

- → The plan? They would guide him to a nearby river for a ground extraction.
- → The challenge? He was deep behind enemy lines.

They had to steer him toward escape — quietly, covertly. Every syllable a tripwire — the North Vietnamese locked on their frequency, waiting for a single wrong breath to blow it all apart. Now the game had changed. And Bat 21? He was about to outplay death.

The Rescue That Defied Logic

When brute force failed, genius stepped in. One of the rescuers — part strategist, part war-born codebreaker — remembered a key detail about Hambleton: the man loved golf. The kind of love that memorizes every course, every hole, every par, and hazard like scripture. So they built a code. Not military code. Not encryption. Recreation turned reconnaissance. Golf turned into a weapon.

"Play the 1st hole at Tucson National" wasn't radio chatter — it was a compass bearing. A calculated lifeline dressed up as Sunday leisure. Each hole gave him distance and direction, and a new language was born — one that slipped past the enemy and spoke straight to a man clawing his way through carnage.

For days, Hambleton played a one-man Masters — except the gallery wasn't clapping. It was death chambering another round. He didn't walk the course — he crawled it like it was a par 3 at Augusta National set on fire. Every step was a silent refusal to be erased. No trophies. No green jacket. Just sweat, hunger, and the roar of war on his heels — a death-grip march to steal the pen from the enemy's hand before it wrote his final chapter. And then — at the edge of collapse, body wrecked — he reached the extraction point. The impossible became history.

This wasn't a standard-issue rescue. This was the biggest, most complex, and most costly search-and-rescue mission of the entire Vietnam War. And it didn't end with an airstrike. It ended with a man who crawled out of death's shadow and a team who made sure that shadow never got the last word. They didn't just bring him home — they redefined what connection, courage, and communication under fire really look like. Because when the map's ash and every rule shatters, your people, your will, and your voice are the only weapons left. And sometimes? They're enough to flip death the bird.

Talk Isn't Cheap

Lt. Col. Hambleton didn't just survive — he became a walking, talking bulletproof receipt for what happens when guts, brains, and balls-out persistence collide with leadership that actually communicates.

Buried beneath the explosions, evasion tactics, and golf-coded wizardry was the real magic: a masterclass in communicating under fire. Literal fire rained down—and they still managed to cut through the noise, sending signals sharper than the bullets slicing the air.

Now you? You've got noise-canceling headphones, color-coded calendars, Wi-Fi, and AI that can outthink most boardrooms. And somehow your team still ends up confused, off-track, and one snark-loaded email away from mutiny.

- → That's not a tools problem.
- → That's a leadership failure.

Gallup—yes, them again, because they're basically the grim reaper of workplace stats—found that only 7 percent of U.S. workers believe communication in their company is accurate, timely, and open.

Seven. Freaking. Percent.

That means the other 93 percent are basically surviving off vibes, poorly punctuated emails, and assumptions dressed up as strategy.

And before you roll your eyes, answer this: if a rescue team can use golf lingo to communicate in a war zone and pull off the most complex rescue to unfold in the entire Vietnam conflict, then what's your excuse for trainwrecking a weekly Ops meeting?

- → Honestly? You don't have one.

Because yeah—you're not ducking shrapnel between budget meetings, but don't act like a blown deadline, a botched rollout, or a missed cue hasn't felt like a PR napalm drop.

The solution? Stop blaming "poor communication" like it's a ghost you can't catch. You're not cursed. You're just not paying attention. It's not the fault of Microsoft Teams or that 47-tabbed project management board you swear by.

It's you. And that's good news — because you can fix you.

Whether you're managing a crisis or just managing to stay employed, naked communication — the raw, uncut, clear-as-day kind — leaves zero room for spin. It's your only shot at leading anything worth remembering.

So pull out your iPad, tablet, or whatever screen you worship and do this — crack open your last comms misfire.

> Where did it skid off the rails?
> What truth did you silence that needed air?
> What part of "We've got a plan" turned into "We've got a problem"?

Let's go full autopsy. No anesthesia. No excuses. Because if you can't name the fracture, you'll keep dressing wounds that never heal. And worse — they don't stay hidden. They follow you. They echo in every new role, every new intro, every "fresh start."

The Sharp End Of Static

Here's the scene: you hit that new role like Tony Stark at a product launch — confidence dialed, AirPods blasting a soundtrack worthy of your entrance. You've studied the org chart, maybe even practiced your "thrilled to be here" smile in the mirror. Then reality smacks you in the face like a rogue dodgeball fired from point-blank range.

Because what no one bothers to mention is that slick intros and surface-level charm don't mean jack when the room is thick with coded body language and landmines disguised as "friendly updates."

And the savage bit? These aren't headline-worthy disasters. They're death by a thousand signal jams. An "I thought you meant…" here, a "Didn't we already discuss that?" there — and poof, your credibility evaporates like a push notification no one even swipes on.

This isn't personal failure — it's static. The background buzz that erodes focus and grinds workplaces down from the inside out.

And the ones who cut through it? They're not louder. They're sharper. Cleaner. Surgical. They wield their words like scalpels. They know instinctively that communication isn't some sidekick propping up leadership — it's mission-critical. Crash it and watch your team blue-screen in real time. No reboot. No patch. No tech saviors riding in. Just silence — and your credibility fried on the motherboard.

Every Word Tilts the Room

Unless you moonlight as a hostage negotiator or have a black belt in conflict resolution, chances are you're winging it. Took a public speaking class back in college? Adorable. That's like bragging you're ready for Navy SEAL training because you once survived a belly flop at summer camp.

Commanding a classroom is child's play. Try leading a shareholder meeting where egos are armed, politics are primed, and every passive-aggressive silence is louder than the agenda. This isn't public speaking — it's psychological warfare with a dress code.

In school, they crammed your head with calculus, the French Revolution, and the periodic table — then sent you out unequipped to navigate landmines like "Per my last email." No crash course on telling the CEO he screwed up without detonating your career. No tutorial on delivering bad news without tanking morale or triggering an HR investigation. Just a diploma, a mountain of student debt, and a ceremonial push into the corporate jungle armed with nothing but vibes, a laptop, and a dream.

So here you are, dodging conversational landmines with a broken compass, a dying flashlight, and an HR handbook that's been collecting dust since the Blackberry era.

And you wonder why everything blows up when someone misreads tone, timing, or tension. Here's what they don't teach you in Leadership 101: communication isn't just another skill on the list — it's the power amplifier, the one that makes every other move hit louder.

So if your messages are landing with all the grace of a flaming piano, it's not a personality flaw — it's a communication blind spot you can fix. Take the meeting that melts down, for example.

> You open with, "Let's talk about what went wrong."
> You mean, "Let's learn from this."
> They hear, "You screwed up."

Defensiveness spikes, insight dies, and the lesson gets lost in the confusion. That's how fast intention derails into interpretation. And it's not just meetings — it's everywhere.

So zoom out and look globally. Where's your blind spot — the moment when your meaning and their understanding veer off like two drunk drivers on parallel roads? Spot it, grab it by the collar, and rewrite the outcome.

Because once you master how to land words with precision, you stop managing impressions—and start bending reality. And on this battlefield, the one who commands the narrative owns the future.

The Language of Leverage

In the corporate jungle, straight talk isn't just a skill—it's a game-changing advantage. It's the catalyst that turns confusion into hell-yes direction, hesitation into hellbent execution, and a room full of doubters into die-hard disciples.

When you're not just pitching an idea—you're fighting for relevance, and the room's already voting with their eyes—remember this: one well-timed curveball can hijack a meeting, flip the vibe, and rewrite the ending.

Picture it: your idea's flatlining in real time. Eyes glazed. Phones out. People are more interested in what's for lunch than your message. What do you do?

Option one:	**Option two:**
Jolt them. Drop a curveball like, "Alright, let's get weird for a second." Boom. Pulse check. Curiosity spikes. And suddenly, it's not "Why should we care?"—it's "What's next?"	Flip the script and go silent. Let the pause stretch just long enough for heads to snap up like they just missed the punchline. Silence isn't absence; it's a power move.

Great communicators don't just talk—they bend time. They play with presence. They twist energy. They wake people up, shift perspectives, and make ideas impossible to ignore.

But let's kill the fantasy — it's not magic. It's muscle. You don't find it at a weekend retreat with complimentary croissants. You build it daily — by sweating through practice, bombing, reworking it, and showing back up sharper.

Look at Hambleton. The man didn't wing it — he recalibrated under fire every single day. That's the game. Because communication today? It's a shapeshifter: remote work, meme-speak, time zones, emoji diplomacy. Hundreds of message channels, each with its own code — and if you don't learn the language of it all, you're toast.

Mind Over Muscle: Train The Beast

Don't panic. You don't need a glorified YouTube tutorial hosted by some guy named Brogan with a man bun to level up. Start where you are. Tiny tweaks? They're the ticket to massive momentum.

> Every text ping.
> Every email subject line.
> Every side-eye in a team meeting.

All of it is a live round. Your chance to be sharper, bolder, more intentional. So stop waiting for someone to pass the mic — grab it, shatter the dead air, and carve your name into the walls.

So where do you begin?

The beauty is that every leader starts in the same place — by choosing to show up and do the work. You've already got the hardware — the original ride-or-die MVP: three pounds of raw processor wired for survival, riding shotgun between your ears. That's your edge. Use it.

Your brain isn't there just to keep you upright and remember your Netflix login. It's a ruthless, round-the-clock rewiring squad. No breaks. No nap time. Just savage adaptation. That's neuroplasticity — the cold, undeniable fact that your brain can rewire, reload, and evolve even after life's sucker punches land square on the jaw.

I didn't skim this out of a book. I lived it. When my mom got hit with an Alzheimer's diagnosis, I didn't retreat. I dove into the deep end of neuroscience and came back swinging with this: the brain isn't fragile glass. It's forged steel with a soft underbelly and an unbreakable will to fight.

Still raising an eyebrow?

Fine. Cue former U.S. Representative Gabby Giffords. In 2011, tragedy struck — one bullet shattered her ability to speak. But she didn't settle for silence. She rebuilt her voice through singing. Note by note. Beat by beat. She wired new neural pathways in her brain and walked back into her power.

That's not just healing — that's neurological warfare with a comeback soundtrack. So the next time your thoughts glitch mid-sentence or your confidence hits the eject button, don't spiral — reboot. You're not broken. You're buffering. Your brain's not the problem — it's the power source.

Of course, even the best systems need direction. Want to turn that gray matter into a guided missile?

Then get deliberate. Train it like the beast it is.

- → Hit the reps.
- → Honor the rest.
- → Then execute — without compromise.

Repetition Rewires: Don't Just Learn It, Burn It In

Reps aren't sexy — but they make you unstoppable. Drill until your words are tattooed into muscle memory. Train your voice in every low-stakes moment so it's lethal in the high-stakes ones. Mastery doesn't come from knowing — it comes from doing again and again until it's impossible to forget.

Rest Resets: Recovery Is a Power Move, Not a Pause

Rest isn't weakness — it's the reset that sharpens instincts, pulls focus out of the fog, and turns exhaustion into precision. You can't out-hustle a fried nervous system. Guard your body like it's mission-critical hardware. Protect your mind like it's classified intel under lock and key. The clearest signals come from leaders who recalibrate — and then move with intent.

Action Sustains: Execute or Evaporate

And when you've recharged? Start training again. Momentum dies in hesitation. Action keeps the beast fed. You don't wait for confidence — you build it in motion. Read as if your impact depends on it. Hunt down conversations that make your palms sweat. Learn a new word and drop it like a Molotov cocktail in the middle of a meeting.

Leaders who dominate the room aren't waiting for perfect conditions — they're armed, ready, and ruthless enough to use every shot they've got. Your brain? Same deal. Locked. Loaded. Waiting for orders. But it won't rewire itself while you're six episodes deep into season 4 of *Bachelor in Paradise*, praying for a vibe shift. This is CrossFit for your cortex — emotional deadlifts, mental bruises, and the "what the actual hell?" that becomes "oh, this is what influence feels like."

> So flex the reps. Hard.
> Recover — then reload and fire again.
> Move like hesitation is fatal.
> Grow like comfort is the enemy.

And never forget: perfection is a fairy tale for the fragile — conquest is what your brain was built for. And that means being able to spot the hustle — because every mental decoy is primed to take you out.

The House Always Wins

Every conversation is rigged before you open your mouth, because bias is the dealer — and the house always wins. Think you're immune? That's bias at peak performance — convincing you this entire section applies to someone else.

That's the delusion — you're *not* immune. It's baked into your DNA like bad code, whispering through every thought, reaction, and "gut instinct" you've ever trusted.

So let's talk about how this tricky little devil actually operates. Your brain, for all its brilliance, is sly. It distorts. It decorates. It feeds you lies dressed in logic and calls it intuition. That's cognitive bias — not just some psychology-class footnote but a trickster running a hustle on your judgment.

The worst part? It doesn't flash red; it feels right, familiar, safe — because it wears the face of your past wins. It whispers validation while it's quietly rigging your next mistake.

Left unchecked, bias will wreck you, dull your instincts, and tank your credibility before you can even draft an apology email. If you want to be a savage-level communicator, start by getting real with your blind spots and assumptions. Gut-check the facts. Because mastery isn't just what you say — it's making sure it's real.

Here's your hit list — the most common mental thugs screwing with your signal:

The Halo Effect

What is it:

It's not just common — it's damn near institutionalized. One shiny trait, like charisma or confidence, hijacks the spotlight and blinds you to the wreckage — mediocrity, toxicity, incompetence simmering just out of frame.

Why it's dangerous:

Some cultures are so hooked on this bias, they've rebranded it as "executive presence." It warps judgment in the moments leaders can't afford distortion — handing power to empty suits and leaving real competence silenced in the corner.

Leaders fall for it every time they:
- Promote the "shiny" high performer who burns bridges.
- Overlook toxic behaviors because results are high.
- Crown a leader for one big win — not their leadership.

Neutralize it: Break it down. Separate who someone *is* from what they actually produce and how they lead.

Confirmation Bias

What it is:

Your brain hunts for proof you're right and dumps what doesn't fit — ego on cruise control while the check-engine light blinks red.

Why it's dangerous:

You stop learning. You defend garbage ideas. You build a leadership bubble that reflects you, not reality. You don't just miss the warning signs — you floor it into the wall, swearing the GPS glitched. You treat filtered data like truth, never realizing the evidence was rigged from the start.

Leaders fall for it every time they:

- Hold strategy sessions that shut down dissent.
- Dismiss opposing views as "negative."
- Treat data like a highlighter, not a microscope.
- Say "I have a gut feeling" and call it instinct.

Neutralize it: Build a culture where healthy disagreement isn't danger — it's data. If every voice echoes yours, you're not leading a team — you're running a fan club.

Bandwagon Effect

What it is:

When the crowd moves, your brain wants to follow — swapping critical thought for consensus.

Why it's dangerous:

It strangles innovation. Yes-men multiply. Ideas get diluted. Groupthink masquerades as alignment. Pressure to "go with the flow" steamrolls judgment, and leaders end up passengers on a runaway train.

Leaders fall for it every time they:

- Follow the trend without checking the fit.
- Avoid rocking the boat to mitigate risk.
- Reward groupthink and label dissent as drama.
- Mimic trends without context.

Neutralize it: Build a team that challenges you, not flatters you. Hunt for what's missing before you sign off. That's where breakthroughs are born.

Dunning-Kruger Effect

What it is:

Leaders and employees with shallow knowledge overestimate their skills, turning them into false prophets — and no one calls them out — cue the YouTube "experts." Meanwhile, the truly skilled stay quiet.

Why it's dangerous:

You promote confidence over competence, and suddenly the loudest, least qualified voice becomes the oracle while the real talent stays invisible. Bad calls pile up. Quiet experts walk. And the culture tilts toward bravado over brains — until your bench is nothing but inflated egos running on fumes.

Leaders fall for it every time they:

- Make bad decisions with unearned confidence.
- Promote the loudest person in the room.
- Overlook quiet experts who actually know their stuff.
- Assume "I've been doing this for years" equals mastery.

Neutralize it: Separate ego from evidence. Create skill-based assessments, not just vibe checks. Value curiosity as much as certainty. Normalize learning and feedback.

Availability Bias:

What it is:

This bad boy is a mental shortcut where your brain mistakes what's loud for what's likely. If it's vivid, emotional, or easy to recall, your brain inflates its importance — no matter how rare it actually is. Drama hijacks your judgment (hello, shark attacks).

Why it's dangerous:
You start reacting to noise instead of patterns. Decisions get hijacked by fear and adrenaline. Meanwhile, quiet talent gets steamrolled, strategy devolves into panic management, and real risks stay buried — silent and invisible until it's too late. Headlines become your holy text, and before you know it, you're leading from clickbait instead of cold, hard reality.

Leaders fall for it every time they:
- Make decisions based on the most recent crisis.
- Let emotional stories override hard data.
- Think one loud complaint equals a trend.
- Obsess over what's urgent and ignore what's important.

Neutralize it: Pause. Gather details. Ask better questions. Go deeper. Then decide. Let data drive direction — not drama.

So next time everything feels just a little off — like the truth's playing hide and seek — stop. Take a breath. What you see might not be fact; it might be bias, dressed in certainty and strutting like it owns the place. Your brain is a genius wrapped in illusions, and the only way to beat it is to stare it down.

Awareness is your flashlight — use it. Shine it into the corners, expose the distortion, then pass it around. Bias doesn't ask for permission — it just takes over. But the second you see it? You take back control.

Need proof? Look back at Hambleton's rescue. Nobody choked. Nobody bowed to protocol or ego. They looked past the conventional, trusted the unthinkable, and coded golf shots in a warzone. And it worked. That's what happens when bias loses its grip.

Check Your Ego or Wreck Your Team

I think it's clear — bias is bad. But ego? Ego's a full-blown assassin. It doesn't just blur the lens — it blinds you, straps you in, and floors it straight into delusion. Ego whispers, "You're crushing it," while the ground caves beneath your team's feet.

And you? You don't see the cracks — you're too busy admiring your reflection in the rearview.

The ugly truth no one admits: ego will gas you up while everything worth leading burns behind you. It flatters. It filters. It feeds you cotton-candy lies while your credibility rots — and the worst part? It feels good. That's the trap. Ego's seductive, but it's a saboteur.

The fact is, influential leadership doesn't live in brilliance or bravado — it lives in impact. The kind that stalks the room long after you're gone. Anyone can make a splash; it's gone in seconds. But the ripple? That's the current they can't escape. That's legacy.

And remember — it wasn't some chest-thumping commander who sparked Hambleton's rescue. It was airmen — focused and ego-free enough to toss the manual and lead with instinct and courage.

So stop pretending ego's just an overactive sense of pride. It's a virus in pinstripes — a silent killer that guts your team and drains the fight right out of them. Left unchecked, ego doesn't just destroy leaders — it manufactures regret. If you're serious about curb-stomping your ego before it blows up your team from the inside out, start here:

Your Team is Your Mirror — Clean Daily

When things start slipping, don't play whack-a-mole with symptoms. Grab the mirror. Your team's off? So are you. Energy cascades from the top — if they're disengaged, it's time for a hard look at what you're projecting. Ego blinds you to the cracks. Leadership demands you face them — and fix them. Growth is the goal. Feedback is the fuel.

Feedback Without Spin

Forget the hollow "Nice job!" crap. Ask your people this: "What's one thing I could do better to help you succeed?" Then shut your mouth and take the hit. That's not weakness — it's the frontline of growth. Your comfort zone is a padded cell. Get out of it.

Confidence Fuels. Ego Chokes

Confidence leads with open hands. Ego leads with a fist. One inspires. One suffocates. If your people are performing out of fear, you're not leading — you're intimidating. That's not respect. That's submission. Check yourself. Reset the vibe.

Less Talk. More Teeth

Stop the posturing. Your actions? They're the billboard. Your people aren't just watching your words; they're also watching your moves. Consistency builds trust. Excuses erode it. Walk the talk until the floorboards remember your footsteps. That's how you build influence that sticks.

It's Your Move

You've hacked through the jungle — called out bias, trained your brain, and sharpened your words into weapons. But insight without action? That's flexing with no weight on the bar — it changes nothing. Knowledge sitting idle is dead weight, and this game's played in real time. With real people. And real stakes.

Lt. Colonel Hambleton didn't sit around waiting for a flawless rescue to drop from the heavens. He bled for every inch. Crawled through hell. Starved in silence. Clung to golf codes like lifelines in a war zone. He didn't just follow strategy — he became the strategy.

And you? Still ducking behind "let's circle back" and "just following up"? That's not leadership. That's verbal camouflage. Leaders don't hedge. They deliver — with weight, with precision.

Stop masking hesitation with polite maybes, watered-down words, and permission slips that will never hit your desk. The best don't ask. They move with intent. They own the room. That's the line between placeholders and powerhouses — only one leaves the room unshaken, undeniable, unforgettable.

So shatter the silence, say what everyone else is too scared to, and when the dust clears, don't just prove you can lead the conversation.

Prove you were born for it.

Naked Awareness

COMMANDING EMOTIONAL INTELLIGENCE

"Emotional intelligence lives in that razor-thin moment
between chaos and clarity, when you get to decide—react
like the world expects or lead like the world needs."

MONA VOGELE

The Power Of The Pause

Life's a relentless brawler — swinging wild, wrecking plans, shredding expectations, and turning your roadmap into confetti. One minute you're cruising; the next, betrayal ambushes you from a blind spot you didn't even know existed. You can't always control the hit — but you damn sure own the response.

→ And that ownership? It lives in the pause.

Not the drawn-out, awkward kind. That nanosecond of pure choice wedged between the trigger and the explosion. That razor-thin space where everything hangs in the balance.

Most people blow right past it, slamming into knee-jerk reactions like a demolition derby of bad choices. But leaders worth remembering? They live there. Not for applause but for influence — forged in the crucible of that stillness. In the white-hot seconds after the hit, when every instinct screams to rage, retreat, or retaliate.

But anyone can react. Hell, a toddler can throw a tantrum. But a leader? A real leader? They don't react. They respond — with purpose and precision.

They seize that split second and wield it like a sword. Not the shiny kind you'd hang above your fireplace, but the kind that's been sharpened in the dark by all the battles you've already fought and walked away from.

And the beauty of the pause? It's always within reach. Whether cornered by circumstances or feeling as insignificant as a penny on the pavement, the power to choose our response sits quietly in our back pocket, waiting for us to have the guts to use it.

Forget the hashtag wisdom — the bumper-sticker quotes, the "just breathe" clichés — ***the pause isn't passive.***

It's a live wire if you've got the nerve to grab it. A full-blown rebellion. A mutiny against your own reflexes. It's the place where you become more than a title, more than your track record, more than your last mistake. It's where you become the one they remember — not for how loud you were but for how deeply you owned the silence.

This isn't about hesitation. It's about dominion. It's a power shift. It's about choosing grace when fury is easier. Resolve when vengeance is louder. Silence — when ego wants a mic drop.

But mastering the pause takes more than sheer willpower. It demands emotional intelligence — the kind that doesn't come from a spreadsheet or seminar. It demands you know your own landmines, feel the detonation coming, and still choose intention over impulse.

In that sliver of stillness lies your legacy.

So take the pause. Sharpen it. Wield it. And lead with the kind of certainty that silences the doubters.

Emotional Intelligence: The Leadership Mixtape

Over the years, I've learned that the loudest voice in the room isn't always the leader. It's not the résumé stacker. It's not the LinkedIn peacock. That's EQ's turf.

Emotional intelligence — the thing that separates the heavy-hitters from the headline-chasers. It's the lethal combo of internal control and external precision — the ability to read the room while your own emotional freight train is trying to derail. Call it whatever you want — EQ's not background music. It's a killer mixtape with a bassline that rattles the room. And once Track One drops? Nobody walks out the same.

Track One: Self-Awareness

This isn't whispering affirmations over kale smoothies or journaling under moonlight like a tortured poet. It's knowing exactly what flips your switch, what lights you up, and what turns you into a live grenade the second someone slips a backhanded compliment into a project update. Self-awareness is the opener to your internal playlist — the track that either fuels your rise or blows without warning.

And if you don't know your triggers, you *are* your triggers. That's not leading — it's just a reflex in a pressed suit waiting to detonate the moment someone smirks in your direction.

But awareness? That's the real flex. When the heat rises and you choose not to combust — there's power in that pause. It's why self-awareness is Track One — because you can't lead anyone else if you can't lead yourself. Know your triggers. Take control before they own you. Then slide into Track Two — self-regulation, where control stops being wishful thinking and starts being your weapon.

Track Two: Self-Regulation

Self-regulation isn't monk-like calm or trying to keep rage corked until it eventually explodes. It means rerouting your fuse — holding the line when you're two seconds from saying what HR would frame as "career-limiting."

And it's not just your words on the line — your face talks too. One eye-roll, one raised eyebrow can say more than a tirade ever could.

Think of it like this: every time you lose it, someone pushed a button. Now imagine if that button didn't even exist.

> No button.
> No detour into damage control.
> No "I probably shouldn't have said that" hangover.

That's what emotional control really looks like — quiet power that doesn't need an audience. And no, it's not natural. It's trained. Rep by sweaty rep. Journal it. Walk it off. Spit it out with someone who gets it. Whatever it takes.

The key isn't burying the rage — it's leading through it. That's the strategy in high-stakes leadership. IQ can crunch equations, but EQ? That's the metric for the messiest puzzle of all — humans. Starting with the one staring back at you in the mirror.

Track Three: Motivation

Motivation isn't a vibe. It's voltage. It's the current running through your veins when the calendar feels like a graveyard of deadlines and your to-do list reads like a Tolstoy novel with a grudge.

But let's be clear: motivation isn't hype. It's not a 6 a.m. gym selfie with earbuds blasting a playlist that promises willpower it can't deliver. That's noise. Real motivation comes from your why — the hair-raising reason you haven't walked off the field even when everyone else did.

This is where emotional intelligence stops being cute and starts cutting deep. Your why is the spark; EQ is the wiring that keeps the system from blowing out. It filters the noise, steadies the pulse, and keeps you from mistaking adrenaline for purpose.

Know this: hype fades — your why doesn't. Motivation without EQ is loud until it dies. But motivation with EQ, anchored to your why? That's bloodline destiny. It doesn't need a spotlight or validation to survive. It's coded into you — and when you lead from that place, people don't just follow; they become proof that destiny scales, and no spreadsheet on earth can measure it.

Track Four: Empathy and Compassion

Empathy is one of the core tracks in emotional intelligence — a frequency every leader needs to master. But with true EQ, leaders can't stop there. Understanding what someone's feeling is powerful, yes, but sometimes the moment demands more than resonance — it demands action.

And when it does, that's where compassion steps in.

Empathy — it's the mirror.

You feel what they feel — their joy, their fear, their wreckage — and it reflects straight back into you. But empathy isn't just sentiment — it's proximity. It's the nerve to stand close enough to someone's fire that you feel the heat.

Compassion — it's the bridge.

You don't just feel it — you move. Compassion in leadership isn't performative kindness; it's the leader who notices the crack in someone's armor and doesn't just nod knowingly but shifts the load, changes the system, or shields the hit. Compassion is empathy with scorch-proof skin — it walks into the fire and refuses to leave anyone behind.

One absorbs. The other acts. And great leaders understand the power in both.

But too often, empathy and compassion get shoved aside like they're the slow ballad on a power playlist — too soft, too tender, too emotional. That's the lie. They're not dragging down the tempo. They *are* the tempo. The pulse your team feels in every corner of the room. Lose them and you're not leading. You're a rerun of bad leadership everyone's seen — and nobody sticks around to watch.

Here's the part the leadership gurus never touch: they sell resilience like it's a magic shield — bounce back, toughen up, grind again. Sure, resilience is staying in the fight — but real strength? That's choosing *how* you fight without surrendering the mission.

> → Empathy and compassion? They flow both ways.

And sometimes, they show up when you least expect them. I'll never forget the day someone on my team locked eyes with me and quietly asked, "Are you okay?" Just three words — small enough to whisper, heavy enough to hit hard. They didn't just crack me — they gutted me.

Because I wasn't. Not even close. They didn't know I was drowning — barely breathing under the weight of watching Alzheimer's erase my mom one cruel memory at a time. I thought the mask was airtight. Turns out I was leaking pain like a busted pipe behind drywall.

EQ isn't just about reading someone else's feelings — it's about being raw enough to admit your own. To say, "I can't carry this alone." The second I let my team in, everything shifted. We weren't just coworkers anymore — we were a tribe bound by truth, not job titles.

That was empathy: they saw me, they felt me, they called out what I was trying to hide.

Then came compassion: they didn't leave me broken on the floor. They carried part of the weight. They adjusted, shielded, and closed ranks so I didn't have to fight alone.

That's empathy and compassion fused. No gimmicks. No lip service. A blade sharp enough to shred through the performative BS and build trust faster than a hundred forced happy hours ever could.

In today's transactional world, empathy and compassion aren't extras — they're the fuel of influential leadership. While everyone else is peacocking for power, this duo walks in unarmed, dripping with sincerity, and leaves fingerprints nobody can erase.

Track Five: Adaptability

Leadership doesn't come with a script — it's improv at full tilt. Plans get incinerated, timelines shredded, and every pair of eyes snaps to you, thinking, "Well, what now?" That's when adaptability walks in — EQ laced with brass knuckles and zero apologies. No outline, no teleprompter — just you and the onslaught you're about to bend into submission.

The leaders who get this don't wait for perfect conditions. They rise from the rubble, scan the wreckage, and — with zero hesitation — say, "Pivot. Now."

Adaptability is locking into your center and refusing to flinch. Because life won't wait for your well-thought-out plan — it'll shove you headfirst into the deep end, then have the nerve to ask if you brought a swimsuit.

And in that moment, you've got two choices: quit — or show up swinging with purpose when everything in you says not to. To keep delivering — not because the stage is set or the conditions are right, but because the mission demands it. Because people are counting on you. Because walking off isn't an option when the weight of what matters most is on the line.

Don't mistake this for simply being flexible — it's ferocity unleashed. That's leadership in motion. The kind that lives in courage — and answers back when the whole room forgets how to breathe.

> It's calling an audible at the 11th hour.
> It's rewriting the map mid-journey.
> It's crafting a new plan on the back of a napkin.

The survival code? Reading the room, feeling the shift, and steering your people forward like this was the plan all along. Because in the end, adaptability isn't a skill. It's a stance. It's leading naked: no script, no safety net — just the ruthless decision to declare, "This isn't the end" and pivot while everyone else folds.

Track Six: Social Skills Greatest Hits

Social skills aren't background vocals — they're the bangers on your mixtape that make people either vibe with you or vanish. This is what separates the charmers from the commanders.

You walk into a meeting that feels like a bar fight's about to break — half the room nursing grudges, the other half gripping imaginary bottles. You don't roll in with bullet points and fake pep. You read the air. You clock the silence. You feel the static in their shoulders. Then you move — steady, surgical, shifting the current with every word.

That's **persuasion** and **influence** at work — the art of bending the room without them realizing it. It's the weight behind your words that shifts the temperature. Presence so sharp it slices through tension like a hot knife through red tape. You're not just seen — you're felt.

Then comes the next evolution — **communication**. Not the manicured "circling back on this" energy. This is speaking with such precision, the room gets yanked out of distraction and straight into you.

Next up: conflict. And if you flinch at the word, the power's already shifted — and not in your favor. Conflict is inevitable with passionate teams — it's the pressure point where things either crack or become legendary. Real leaders don't dodge it — they turn that tension into traction. That's **conflict management** with the gloves off.

Then the remix hits: **change management**. Deadlines shift. Priorities lurch sideways. The whole terrain tilts. But you? You're already plotting your next move. Because change doesn't rattle you — it gives you a stage to prove you can lead without cue cards.

And just when they think you've peaked? You drop **collaboration** like an amplifier at max volume. Not some phoned-in "can I get your thoughts?" email at 4:59 p.m. on a Friday. This is shoulder-to-shoulder execution. The kind that builds momentum you can feel in your chest. No weak links. No dead weight. Just a crew moving with impact.

And underneath it all — **relationships**. Not small talk or fake empathy. I'm talking about trench-deep loyalty. The 3 a.m. calls.

The unvarnished hits. The kind of bond that doesn't need a calendar invite. These connections don't just support the mission — they're rooted deep in the soil where real leadership grows.

EQ: The Echo That Endures

You can't fake your way into it. EQ demands receipts. Proof you've stood in the dark with your fear, stared it down, and walked through it anyway. Not perfection — precision. Not pretending — truth, even when lies would be easier. Not bulletproof — real and unafraid to be seen that way.

Now slam the brakes. Think about the last time frustration had its hands around your throat — rage in the driver's seat. The shift is choosing clarity over combustion. That clarity builds trust — and trust is where authenticity takes root. That's the quiet power that steadies the room when everyone else is spinning.

Authenticity isn't a veneer people admire — it's the undercurrent that makes them believe before you've even asked. And that belief? It's born of EQ. The earned kind built callous by callous in the space between "I want to quit" and "I'm not done yet."

Because leadership isn't a PR campaign — it's a full-contact sport. You'll get hit. You'll get blindsided by moments that couldn't care less about your résumé. That's where EQ steps in — not as a bonus skill, but as bone-deep truth: influential leadership requires a soul that's unshakable, even when the hit lands hardest.

So walk in with your scars, your fear, your humanity — and lead in a way that creates an echo — long after the project's archived, the inbox is cleared, and the applause has faded.

Take every track of EQ and remix it into your leadership soundtrack. Not a one-hit wonder. Your signature album. The kind that doesn't just chart — it defines an era and stays on repeat until the culture bends to it.

Show up. Stand tall. Own the pause.

Make your leadership ring so loud the echo becomes legend.

Naked Culture

BUILDING A LASTING LEGACY

"Build a culture so irresistible even your competition
wishes they worked for you."

MONA VOGELE

Culture Eats Strategy — Then Licks The Plate

They say, culture eats strategy for breakfast. Accurate? Yeah — but it doesn't stop there. It torches the napkin, flips the table, and orders seconds — with bottomless mimosas — just to make a point.

→ Org chart? Digested.
→ KPIs? A forgotten side dish.

Because culture? It's your entire company's operating system — unfakeable, unseen, and completely in charge.

And guess what? No amount of kombucha on tap or "your voice matters" campaigns will save a team that's silently suffocating. Ping-pong doesn't cover up fear. Beanbags won't mend betrayal.

 **You want the real thing?** Then get out from behind your desk and onto the front lines. Start with the uncomfortable stuff — communication that cuts through the BS. Trust that digs in. EQ that's not performative. Accountability that doesn't blink.

Unsexy, sure — but unshakable at its core, built to outlast every shiny fraud in the room.

The good news straight from Gallup: engaged teams don't just perform — they print money, driving 23 percent more profit. That's not a revenue boost — it's your growth engine. Ignore it, and you're not just bleeding people and profits — you're hemorrhaging relevance.

So take a long, hard look, because your culture's already on display — loud and untamed. Whether your workplace hums like a jazz band or screeches like a chainsaw hitting rebar, that energy starts with you.

Forget the morale patches and hollow "we care" swag — this is a demolition. Blow up the safe zones. Build a culture people fight to stay in and rivals can't replicate. This isn't a vibe shift — it's a cultural uprising. Let's go.

The Unexpected Path

Culture is a sneaky little devil. It's always there, yet somehow invisible. It's like glitter after a kid's birthday party — lodged in your carpet, hiding in your underwear, showing up months later in your morning cereal. You think you've got it handled and then — bam — it's running the show.

But don't confuse "existing" with "intentional." Too often, culture gets duct-taped together with hollow slogans like "Teamwork Makes the Dream Work" and then left to rot faster than that New Year's resolution to stop drunk-texting your ex.

And no, it's not HR's problem to "own." You can't offload it like it's last quarter's swag inventory. It's not pajama Fridays or that sad poster reminding you to "Be the change."

Culture is what shows up when everything else goes up in flames. It's the emotional Velcro that keeps your team from the peace-out parade when crap hits the fan and the paycheck isn't reason enough to stay.

The fiercest culture I've ever laid eyes on didn't come from a billion-dollar budget or a six-month strategic rollout. It came from an airline.

Yeah, a place that's basically a pressure cooker with wings — where folks scream about carry-ons, delays summon the apocalypse, and everyone's hangry by gate B12.

And somehow — *somehow* — it had more heart, humor, and connection than any slick "culture campaign" I'd ever seen.

Still not feeling it? No biggie — pour yourself something strong because we're about to take a hard right into Nashville, where my picture-perfect dream imploded and I got a front-row seat to the kind of spirit that actually changes lives.

Buckle up. We're going in.

From Nashville To A New Calling

The scene: Nashville and me. By day, I was slinging overpriced filet mignon to music execs from a menu so bougie it should have come with a trust fund. The tips were there, but even on a good day, the math never carried me far enough.

By night, I chased neon-lit dreams with nothing in my pockets — and zero backup plan. I was hustling like my rent, my dreams, and my dignity were dangling off the same frayed thread — because let's be real, they were. I didn't just want it — I was starving for it.

Then the plot twist no one expected. And not the cute rom-com kind. This was a sniper shot out of nowhere. One call from Mom. "The doctors say I have Alzheimer's."

And just like that, the music stopped. No slow motion fade-to-black. Just everything inside me collapsing like a house of cards in a hurricane.

I didn't flinch. I packed the fiddle. Shelved the dream and punched a one-way ticket to Dallas. There was no dramatic pause. No weighing the pros and cons.

> Just instinct.
> Just love.
> Just go.

Overnight, I went from chasing gigs to navigating memory tests, appointment hellscapes, and the crushing fog of a disease that steals your person one piece at a time.

The spotlight? Gone. The music? Silent. The stage door slammed, and I was a ghost of the fire I once carried — coasting on fumes and sheer will, praying the tank outlasted the tears.

Music didn't just feel far away. It felt like a fantasy I hallucinated in another lifetime — before life hit back. And then, like all great "WTH?" moments, redemption showed up in the middle of a late-night soul-crack session with a bottle of cheap gas station wine — double pour.

> *"You should work for an airline," my friend tossed out,*
> *deadpan. "Fly for free. Chase the music on weekends."*

I laughed so hard I almost baptized the couch in merlot. It sounded like one of those drunk epiphanies that die with the hangover. But it landed like a lifeline. And something deep in the wreckage — bruised, but not broken — whispered back, "Why the hell not."

More Than a Résumé

Fast forward — I'm stepping into the fevered frenzy of an airport, decked out in my best "hire me, please" outfit, ready to convince

Southwest Airlines that I was more than just another résumé on the pile.

I breezed past the ticket counter — where people actually seemed to enjoy their jobs. It didn't feel like a company; it felt more like a crew. The kind of crew who'd moonwalk to the gate if it meant making someone smile.

Then came the labyrinth of cubicles — high-fives, inside jokes, and caffeine carnage. Eventually, I landed in a conference room with five other hopefuls. Actually, make that six — thanks to a last-minute wildcard who strolled in like she'd just stepped off a reality show.

From the jump, it was clear: this wasn't the standard "tell me about a time" charade. This was *Survivor* meets speed dating in the *Hunger Games* of hiring — and the wrong move could take you out.

At exactly 9 a.m., in rolled three Southwest employees — no suits, no stoic stares. Just khakis, polos, and scuffed sneakers — the kind of crew who'd help you move a couch on a Saturday afternoon, then destroy you at karaoke that night. No robot energy — just people who felt human.

Then their first question: "Tell us something you learned about one of the other candidates while we were out of the room."

BOOM. Game on. Suddenly, this wasn't a skills test — it was a blood test. Not about credentials. Not degrees. Not the alphabet soup after your name or LinkedIn humblebrags.

> Could you make a stranger feel seen?
> Could you really listen?
> Could you make a minute feel like a moment?

If you couldn't lock in, lean in, and elevate the room — thanks for playing, but you were never the one.

Lucky for me, I didn't just read the room — I felt it. I landed the job and a boarding pass into a workplace vibe that didn't just preach values from the C-suite — it flew them at cruising altitude.

The Gospel of No Compromise

That wasn't an interview. That was a full-body character MRI masquerading as one. It didn't ask you to impress — it dared you to be real. Their hiring strategy? Heart over hustle. And it worked — because when business goes off the rails, degrees won't save your team or your company. People and culture will.

Culture doesn't just hire — it reshapes, refines, and straight-up transforms. In a world obsessed with credentials, Southwest bet on mindset. "Hire for attitude, train for skill" wasn't just talked about — it was gospel. And the high priest of that gospel? Herb Kelleher — the founder who knew what was up long before the rest of corporate America caught on.

Herb understood one undeniable fact: skills can be taught, but attitude is rooted in your core — it's either hardwired into your DNA, or it's not. He knew that culture isn't just who you hire — it's who you refuse to hire when compromise comes knocking.

He led like your rock 'n' roll uncle — cigarette in one hand, manifesto in the other — equal parts wild card, wise sage, and Wild Turkey. Herb didn't just build an airline. He built a movement, one irreverent hire at a time.

Now don't get it twisted — some roles absolutely require credentials. You're not handing over the flight deck to someone who just watched a Top Gun montage and felt inspired. Skills matter. No argument there. But culture? It's what builds industry giants while everyone else is building org charts.

Here's where it gets bold — and where most leaders cave. Say two pilots walk in: both certified aces, both capable of getting that metal bird off the ground and back again. But neither has the mindset that fits the culture. Now pile this on: you're short-handed, and every instinct is screaming to fill the gap. What do you do?

You pass — on both. Because the biggest problem isn't an empty Captain's chair — it's the wrong body strapped into it. Hiring talent that doesn't match your DNA? That's a virus that corrodes. A slow leak that eventually floods the entire system.

And that's not easy. But that's what leadership looks like when it refuses to settle for "good enough." Legendary companies don't settle for competent. They aim for magnetic. They hire people who don't just do the job — they become the brand. "Good enough" is the enemy. And Southwest knew that better than anyone.

Building Believers — Not Bystanders

Still think culture is HR's pet project? A warm blanket for fragile morale? Tell that to the companies swinging it like a wrecking ball and leaving the old rulebooks in rubble.

Culture or Cash Out

Zappos doesn't just sling shoes. They sling loyalty — making employee engagement look like a rock concert and a therapy session had a baby. Every year, they hand the mic to their people and say, "Let it rip." No PR spin. Just real talk, unfiltered and undeniable, straight from the team. The result? Culture that isn't curated — it's carved from truth.

And here's the gutsiest move of all: they offer new hires $4,000 to quit if they don't feel the fit. That's not clickbait. That's a cultural throat punch — you're either all in or you cash out. Why? Because they don't want warm bodies — they want lit-up humans ready to build something that matters. When loyalty starts from the inside out, you don't just get retention — you get ride-or-die believers who tattoo your mission onto their mindset. That's not culture as an initiative. That's culture as a lifestyle.

The Haka Effect

The New Zealand All Blacks aren't just a rugby team — they're a leadership factory disguised as one. Their secret weapon? Culture. Every player, from superstar to rookie, lives by one rule: "Leave the jersey better than you found it."

That's not a slogan slapped on a locker room wall — it's the backbone of their dynasty.

They sweep their own locker room after matches. They reject ego, even when they're world champions. They believe character off the field shapes performance on it. And before every game, they unleash the haka — a raw, thunderous war dance that doesn't just intimidate opponents, it unites the team in a living, breathing declaration of identity and purpose.

That culture built one of the most dominant teams in sports history — not because they collect talent, but because they demand humility and loyalty to the mission above everything else.

Build a culture like theirs, and you don't just get compliance — you get conviction. People who don't show up as bystanders, but as believers.

Blood Type: Culture

Southwest, Zappos, the All Blacks — they all figured out what most companies still screw up: culture isn't a strategy. It's blood type.

These brands don't sell products. They sell belief systems. They don't just recruit talent — they anoint. Their people are tribes of fired-up humans sworn to the mission. Their culture is so distinct you can't copy it without looking like a poser. That's the difference between icons and the smoke-and-mirrors crowd — culture that outlives campaigns and burns hotter than optics.

 **You want to lead like these icons?** Then build a culture so potent it wrecks your competitors' sleep and stalks boardrooms you've never even entered.

And for the love of all that's worth fighting for — don't fake it. A knockoff culture is easy to spot. It collapses under pressure, reeks of desperation, and leaves a trail of burned-out employees who stopped believing the minute the catered lunch ran out.

Rogue Power Moves That Win

Culture doesn't need a press release. *It needs proof.* Forget titles — authentic leadership is felt, not framed. If your culture isn't punching through the drywall with your values, then it's just corporate cosplay in business casual.

Google understood that. They didn't invite innovation to the table — they duct-taped a mic to its hand, shoved it on stage, and told it to own the room. Their iconic 20% time wasn't a perk; it was sanctioned rebellion. A green light to dream like a maniac, crash spectacularly, and drag the wreckage into breakthroughs that reshaped the world — Google Maps among them.

That's the payoff when leadership loosens the chokehold and starts handing out oxygen. Culture suffocates in silence. Whatever your people are breathing in carries your scent, for better or worse. And if that air turns toxic, that trail leads straight back to you.

 **You want innovation?** Praise the flops, louder than wins.
You want collaboration? Make success a team sport.
You want engagement? Make the work matter.

Every one of those moves is a deposit. They stack like interest — the compound-trust kind — until your people are betting sweat equity and belief in you. Not because you're perfect, but because your ledger is undeniable.

None of that's in the policy manual — but it damn sure should be. It lives in how you show up when the spotlight's off, how you react when the pressure spikes, and how you handle the weird, uncut moments that even the PR department can't sanitize.

REMEMBER

- Leadership without culture? Ego in a suit.
- Culture without leadership? All vibe, no spine.
- Combine the two? Unhinged momentum.

You're not managing energy — you *are* the energy. Culture lives in the undiluted day-to-day: every laugh, every call you return, every boundary you draw and refuse to let anyone cross. These moments aren't trivial — they're proof. The quiet receipts that tell your team, *yeah, this leader shows up.*

Like the time I commandeered the mic to help an agent at a packed, delayed, and impatient Southwest Airlines gate to Amarillo — and belted out "Amarillo by Morning." Pitch-perfect? Nope. Real? Hell yes. And that moment said more about culture than twenty branding campaigns ever could.

And here's the deal: while you're the architect, culture isn't a solo act — it's a jam session. When everyone's dialed in — from the rookie sweating through his first presentation to the exec sealing deals with authority — that's when the whole place finds its groove.

So ask yourself: Are you phoning it in with worn-out habits, strumming the same tired chords on repeat? Or are you building something so electric, people would fight tooth and nail for a piece of it?

The good news — you don't have to be perfect. You just have to be real. Grind your actions into your values until there's zero daylight between what you preach and what you live. Do that long enough and your culture won't whisper your values — it'll shout them so loud the walls shake.

When Culture Hits Turbulence

For years, I've hyped Southwest Airlines like a rock star at center stage — and they earned every word. They aren't just a carrier — they're *the* culture blueprint in the sky. Their people aren't just background players — they're the heartbeat in branded polos. Culture isn't an afterthought — it's tangible.

But here's the rub — culture keeps a record. It remembers every broken promise, every fake smile, every eye-roll you thought they didn't clock. Eventually, when it cracks, it's never a quiet creak — it's a full-blown decompression. And even the giants aren't immune.

February 2025. For the first time in its history, the airline that built its empire on employee-first values made a move no one saw coming: mass layoffs. Not a gentle "organizational alignment" — just 1,750 corporate employees gone. No graceful fade. Just fallout.

Why the Sudden Descent?

So what happens when the company known for rewriting the culture roadmap suddenly flips the script? Even a high-flier like Southwest isn't immune to headwinds. Rising operational costs. Fierce competition. And now there's a new player in the cockpit: Wall Street.

Enter Elliott Investment Management — a hedge fund with sharp elbows and a reputation for shaking things up. Their game isn't culture — it's cuts, spreadsheets, and squeezing every last drop of ROI. The problem? Culture doesn't make their quarterly reports. And when financial investors smell inefficiency, values get left on the tarmac.

Southwest always said *people first*. Wall Street says, *profits first. Period.* And when those worlds collide, culture is the first thing tossed out the emergency exit.

For decades, Southwest's no-layoff policy wasn't policy at all — it was doctrine, untouchable and absolute. Post-9/11, during COVID, through fuel crises and punishing downturns, they held the line. No pink slips. That wasn't just clever PR spin; it was a cultural standard. A promise that said, "We've got you."

Now, for some, that standard feels broken. And this isn't just about those who were let go. It's also about those who stayed — walking into quieter offices, side-eyeing empty desks, and wondering if the heart of the company they signed up for is still intact.

Because when layoffs morph from last resort to strategy, the fallout isn't logistical — it's personal. Trust takes the first hit. Then identity. Then culture itself.

And for a company that made culture its calling card — those hits land hard.

The Fallout: When Legacy Meets Reality

The announcement didn't just drop — it hit like sudden turbulence at 30,000 feet. No warning. Just impact. Social feeds lit up like a distress flare — shock, confusion. Lifers who'd given decades to the brand spilled gut-punch stories.

And it wasn't just the exit. It was the silence. The swiftness. The sudden severing of a bond that had once felt unbreakable. And the part no one wants to say out loud — but rattled everyone's sense of stability? If the company that preached loyalty louder than anyone can be shoved off course by Wall Street, is anyone safe? When legacy can be overruled by quarterly performance, what's left?

The message is loud, even if it's unspoken: we're in a new era —
one where even the cultural giants can stumble. Not because
they stopped caring, but because they got caught between
values and valuation. This is where leadership gets tested. This is
where culture either collapses — or fights for its life.

The Final Approach: Lessons in the Logbook

Don't dress this up like a tidy case study. This is a warning shot on
approach — no seatbelt sign, no gentle descent. Culture's not your
parachute. It's your wings. The frame holding your people midair
when the sky goes black and the systems start flashing red.

Yes, even the heavyweights get rattled. Even empires hit
crosswinds. But what you do next? That's the story they'll tell.
Trust isn't a perk — it's marrow in the bone. Cut it, and you'd better
have the brass to own it. When you lead with conviction your
people will bend, recover, and rise — but screw it up, and you don't
just bruise morale, you amputate your credibility.

So here's your flight check: are you performing culture — or living
it? Are your values decals on the wall — or war paint on your face?
When the oxygen masks drop and the cabin's shaking, your team
isn't reaching for your earnings report; they're reaching for you.
Don't wait for turbulence to define your culture — if you do, you're
already spiraling. Build it now. Live it out loud. Lead, knowing your
signature's stamped on every outcome.

And to my former Southwest cohorts — the tribe in blue, red,
and gold — you didn't just show me what culture could be. You
embodied it. You lived it with every gate announcement, every
rerouted flight, every moment that made strangers feel like part
of the warrior pack — feral, fierce, and flying tight.

I'm still locked on your frequency — amped, unapologetic, hyping you like rockstars at center stage. That warrior spirit, that fun-loving attitude, that servant's heart? They haven't gone anywhere. They're still there, cutting through turbulence, refusing to go dark.

And I'll never forget the nights when those red-bellied warriors hit the gate, the engines cut, and the cabin fell quiet — the culture still hummed like residual power through steel.

Unseen, but unmistakable.

CHAPTER

Naked Ownership

THE ART OF UNWAVERING ACCOUNTABILITY

"No accountability, no results. Take the reins, or watch everything fall apart—it's that simple."

MONA VOGELE

Accountability: Locking Down Badass Leadership

No big surprise — accountability isn't the sexy, champagne-popping side of leadership. Nobody's posting selfies after a tough conversation with a caption like, "Just owned my failure. #blessed."

Because this part? It's brutal. You can't soft-shoe your way around it. Accountability doesn't camp out in your comfort zone sipping cold brew and firing off polite "circling back" emails. It lives in the underbelly. It's the midnight call where you own what broke. It's the scorching silence you shatter when nobody else will.

Strip away the perks and your corner-office view. What's left — if you're legit — is accountability. The raw, unbreakable kind that doesn't fold when the air gets thick and the room goes ice-cold. It's the vault that keeps the truth intact — the force that stops leadership from collapsing into smoke and mirrors.

This is where leaders are strengthened — not in off-sites with matching polos, but in the sweat-on-your-upper-lip conversations you'd rather crawl out a bathroom window to avoid.

Accountability isn't just about owning the major deviations — it's about catching the tiny drifts before they wreck the whole damn company. If you're not correcting the heading every day, you're not leading. You're babysitting grown adults in a values-branded comfort bubble.

One Degree Drift

Singapore to New York — 9,500 miles. Longest commercial flight on the planet. But drift just one degree off course, and by the time you land, you're not in New York — you're roughly 166 miles off and in the wrong freaking city. That's not arrival — it's failure dressed as "almost." And business doesn't forgive "almost." One weak standard. One "good enough" hire. Each is a one-degree drift. Stack them, and the result doesn't even resemble what you set out to build — it's wreckage wearing your logo.

But drift isn't destiny. You don't need a rescue mission — you need accountability. One standard reinforced. One system rebuilt. One tough call you stop dodging. Each one is a one-degree correction back toward your target. It takes guts to commit to this level of precision: relentless focus on the heading — every decision, every day, no excuses — until you land, not almost, but exactly where you swore you would.

So gut-check yourself. Are you piloting this thing — or drifting 166 miles into irrelevance?

When Culture Stops Pretending

In a culture steeped in accountability, hard conversations aren't considered a nuclear option — they're part of the job. Every day. Every reality you'd rather choke on than say out loud.

You don't earn trust by ignoring the issue and think you're being nice. You earn it by standing in the tension and spitting truth before it guts your integrity. Strong teams don't toss blame like a hot potato. They snatch it bare-handed, take the scorch, and fix it — fast.

And in a culture that's locked on accountability, this becomes instinct. Because friction isn't the enemy — it's the resistance that sharpens you. Dodge it and watch your culture slide into the carousel of stalling, blame, and mediocrity — dressed up as professionalism.

You've seen it. My bet: you've probably lived through it.

And please, let's not pretend — accountability isn't just tested in the boardroom. It's tested in the checkout line, at carpool pickup, over cocktails with your BFF — in the gritty moments nobody posts about. Dodge those long enough and you're not just avoiding discomfort — you've turned accountability into your imaginary friend.

So, how do you make it real? **You. Go. First.**

Real accountability doesn't need a calendar invite. It barges in, looks the moment dead in the eye, and says, "This ends here. Let's do this together." It's not about calling people out — it's about calling them up. It sets the bar — and makes damn sure nobody crawls under it.

> So say the thing.
> In the room.
> While it still matters.

Accountability lives in the conversation that cracks the ground and forces everyone to choose where they stand.

The Crucible of Conversation

Let's kill the myth now: tough conversations aren't some heroic leadership milestone. They're not "growth moments." They're a responsibility — where truth shows up uninvited and dares you to deal with it. This is the spotlight nobody wants — and when it hits, there's nowhere to hide. In that glare, truth moves fast. It exposes who's actually leading and who's just cashing checks with an empty nameplate. These moments don't wait for your confidence to arrive. It's just you, the facts, and whether you've got the juice to own the outcome — or just a list of excuses to hide behind.

Don't fake your way through it. Walk into these moments unprepared, and you're gambling — going all in on a bluff and praying it holds while your people pay the price. One vague sentence. One watered-down deflection. And boom — what could've been solved just became a trust-killing disaster.

Leaders screw this up all the time. They wing it. They "see how it goes." They walk into loaded conversations with zero direction and expect it to land clean. It doesn't.

Influential leaders don't guess. They prepare. Because clarity isn't built on your tired praise–criticism–praise sandwich. Your team can't own what they don't understand. If they don't know what's working, what's broken, and where things are going, you're not communicating — you've reduced leadership to a glorified guessing game with nothing to chew on but confusion.

→   The harsh truth? Ambiguity is where accountability dies.

Want to avoid the spiral? Get precise. And before you even think about opening your mouth, lock this down:

> What's the actual issue?
> What does progress look like right now?
> What does "we fixed it" look like long-term?

Drive it home. Precision isn't just your best shot — it's your only shot.

From Words to Results

It's no secret — high-stakes confrontations are intense, fueled by emotion, and one shaky breath away from implosion. That's why most leaders either dodge the moment entirely or bulldoze through it. Sadly, both options backfire. One leaves your team confused. The other leaves them traumatized.

The pros don't wing it or stumble in half-cocked. They pause. They read the room. They strip their own baggage at the door and step in clear. No guesses. No gambling. Just focus.

And when the tension thickens? They don't dance around it. They name it. They drag it into daylight and tie it back to the mission — so no one forgets what matters.

But they don't stop there. They don't just "process feelings" and float out lighter — they create movement, ownership, a fix. Otherwise, it's just scheduled whining with better vocabulary.

Look — fear isn't the enemy. Avoidance is. You can't out-lead what you won't confront. Step into it fully, with clarity, and you rewire how your people see accountability — not as punishment, but as the standard, owned and enforced by everyone.

So here's your play:

> Step in.
> Stay in.
> Make it unmistakable.
> Drive it home.

Because if you want to lead something unforgettable, you've got to choose deliberate discomfort — and stay there until it takes hold.

Stay in the Heat: Where Alignment Lives

Even when you prep like a pro, these conversations can spin out faster than a GPS in a tunnel — one wrong turn and you're off course.

The key? Forget trying to "win." You're not redlining through the Daytona 500, praying your tires don't melt before the turn. But you *are* in the driver's seat — and the goal isn't domination. It's direction. Steering through the pack when everyone else starts to lose traction.

Here's how the pros hold the line:

Call It Out

If the conversation wobbles, say it: "We're stuck — how do we fix this?" Shift focus from blame to solutions.

Refocus on the Mission

Ask, "What's the big picture here?" When both sides see the shared goal, the detours start to make sense.

Collaborate, Don't Dominate

It's a duet, not a solo. Aim for harmony. In leadership, control is cheap — but trust is everything.

Experience taught me this — achieving alignment isn't clean or pretty. And it sure as hell isn't comfortable. But it's everything. It's the kind of groove that only shows up when both sides drop the ego, lean into the sting, and choose progress over pride.

And yeah, sometimes you'll fumble it. You'll say something off-base. They'll shut down, and the silence starts to set in.

> Don't run.
> Don't retreat.
> Don't default to damage control.

Stay in it. Adjust. Own your part. Drag the conversation back on track with less "I'm right" energy and more intention. That's leadership — staying planted in the discomfort when every nerve screams to bail. Choosing dialogue over disappearing.

> That's how cracks turn into rebuilds.
> That's how teams relearn trust.
> That's how leaders turn presence into permanence.

The Payoff: Fear In, Fire Out

We've done the hard part — gutted the excuses, faced the mirror, called out ambiguity — it's time for the payoff: what you get when you stop tiptoeing around the discomfort and actually lead through it.

Tough conversations? They're not landmines. They're catalysts. The exact moment trust stops being hot air and starts pulsing in the room. The place where accountability grows muscle and culture bares its teeth.

This isn't just leadership — it's strategic backbone. It's where average leaders tap out and the bold ones step in. Just raw intention and the guts to stay planted when tension seizes the room. It's not comfortable, but it's real — and incredibly rare.

Done right, hard conversations don't fracture teams — they make them bulletproof. They don't bruise your credibility — they forge the kind of leader people would follow through hell and back. So stop circling the issue and drag it into the light. Stand in it, stay in it, and hold the line — because in those unrehearsed, skin-in-the-game moments, leadership proves it can carry the weight.

The Ugly Truth About Avoidance

Avoidance always leaves a mark. Cracks don't stay hairline — they split, and when they do, the fallout is brutal and usually public. Companies don't crumble because of one bad quarter; they implode because leaders chose silence over truth. Delay over decision. Comfort over confrontation. And eventually the bill comes due.

When Vision Turns Viral

Take Theranos. In 2003, it burst onto the scene like a lab-coat fairy tale — a blood-testing startup promising to rewrite the rules with a single drop. In practice? A masterclass in how charisma, ambition, and unchecked ego can hijack an entire system.

While investors poured in millions and patients rolled up their sleeves, Elizabeth Holmes built an empire on illusion. Lab results were faked. Machines malfunctioned. Lives were toyed with. And through it all? The company doubled down on denial — sealing labs, silencing whistleblowers, and selling hype like it was hope.

The result? A billion-dollar collapse, criminal convictions, and a founder sentenced to 11 years behind bars. The investors vanished, the dream imploded, and the company that once promised to "change the world" became a global punchline.

Because accountability shows up — whether you invite it or not. And when it does, it doesn't care about your vision deck, your valuation, or your press quotes. It comes to collect. Theranos wasn't killed by technology; it was buried by the arrogance of leaders who thought accountability was optional.

Tarnished in Trash Can Code

The Houston Astros, 2017. On paper, they won the World Series. In reality? They rigged it — surveillance cameras in the outfield, trash cans banging signals like a back-alley hustle, and a cheat system so blatant it turned the game into a con job.

When the story broke in 2019, it didn't unravel — it exploded. Fans foamed. Players raged. Politicians piled on. Calls to strip the title echoed everywhere.

And the league's response? A shrug dressed up as punishment — fines, a few draft picks docked. The team's manager and general manager were suspended for a year, eventually fired by the owners. But the players? Untouched. No suspensions. No missed games. No lost rings. In MLB, that wasn't punishment — it was PR.

The Astros kept the trophy — but without real accountability, they forfeited the one thing you can't hoist, buy, or fake: legitimacy. You can win on paper and still lose everything that matters.

> The trust of your peers.
> The respect of your industry.
> The heart of your story.

Yeah, they've still got die-hard fans chanting long after the fallout, defending every swing. But the sting's still fresh — for every player robbed and every fan who once believed. And the Astros? Their legacy will always wear an asterisk — bold, permanent, and loud.

The Anatomy of Avoidance

Every collapse starts the same way — not with sirens or scandal, but with silence. A shady call ignored. A boundary crossed and brushed off. A conversation ducked — again and again. The rot sets in quietly, manageable at first — wrapped in polite language and labeled "business as usual." But don't be fooled — that's just the first crack.

Because silence doesn't stay still. It spreads. It learns your habits. It slips into meetings, hallways, inboxes — armed with a clipboard and clichés — and we let it. We defend it. Excuse it. Until one day, it stops knocking altogether — and kicks the door off its hinges.

- → Trust? Vaporized.
- → Credibility? Warped beyond repair.
- → Culture? Twisted into something unrecognizable.

You want to know what really sinks teams and topples dynasties: not scandal, not sabotage.

Avoidance.

And it spreads like rust under fresh paint. It's leadership corrosion in disguise — the passive-aggressive cousin of anarchy. A thousand paper cuts that bleed out belief, one sidestep after another.

By the time you smell the smoke, the fire's already five rooms deep and eating the floor out from under you. That's when the fire stops being a metaphor — and starts burning through your reputation.

When it comes to accountability, you're faced with two choices. Step into the heat and own it, or dodge it and burn with it. There's no middle ground, no balcony seat where you can watch your credibility collapse while pretending you're not in the blast zone.

Whether you struck the match or just let the embers smolder, the outcome's the same: the fire comes — and it consumes everything. The systems. The belief people had in you. The trust you took years to build and seconds to betray.

Leadership doesn't wait. Legacy doesn't pause. Alignment is everything. When your message and your behavior don't sync, your leadership is nothing more than a con. And cons don't fade quietly. They implode — dragging everything with them.

Feedback And Vulnerability: The Power Duo

If avoidance is what destroys your leadership from the inside, feedback and vulnerability are how you drag it back from the grave — wiser and ready to rebuild. This isn't some feel-good combo wrapped in soft skills. It's your comeback cocktail — and it burns going down.

Feedback gives people direction. Vulnerability gives them permission. Together, they haul credibility out of the gutter and inject the kind of leadership your team's been starving for. Because if your people can't tell you the truth, they'll tell it somewhere else — and you won't like where it lands.

But brace yourself — feedback stings. It's the jolt you never asked for: it drops you flat for a beat, then kicks you back to life sharper than before. Skip it and you don't just dodge discomfort — you're spoon-feeding complacency like it's all-you-can-eat night.

→ But feedback alone? Dead on arrival.

It only lands if you've got the stones to sit in the sting without reaching for excuses or your title. Growth demands vulnerability —

the courage to hear what you'd rather ignore and the backbone to do something about it. That's the line in the sand. Leaders adjust. Performers defend. Vulnerability isn't about tears in a town hall or an over-rehearsed "I take full responsibility" monologue. It's showing up, stripped of spin, and proving that accountability isn't just for everyone else.

You want a feedback culture that actually delivers? Normalize it. Make honesty as common as caffeine. Kill the awkward "we need to talk" rituals and build real-deal feedback loops — constant, two-way, unfiltered.

This is where blind spots get exposed and growth becomes a baseline — not a bonus. So make it count. Use the feedback. Let vulnerability lead. Don't chase perfection — chase progress. That's how cultures rise and how leaders build influence.

Execution or Extinction

You can run all the feedback sessions, huddles, and pep talks in the world — but if nothing changes, congratulations: you've built yourself a hamster wheel with better lighting.

→ Words without decisive action? Worthless.

And the cost of inaction? Way higher than most leaders are willing to pay. Productivity and momentum flatline. Your team shows up in body — but their belief? Already gone. And once belief walks out the door, performance isn't far behind. It follows like a shadow.

People don't trust what you *say*. They trust what you repeat. What you reinforce. What you hold people accountable for. So, before the conversation ends and anyone leaves the room, accountability gets specific.

Who's on the hook?

Names on tasks. No exceptions. "We'll figure it out later" is leadership's favorite lie — don't let it sneak in. If it's everyone's job, it's no one's job.

When's it due?

Set deadlines. Without them, you're in the land of eternal "maybe," where good ideas go to die and accountability goes into witness protection.

What's the follow-up?

Progress doesn't track itself. This isn't micromanaging — confirm, don't assume. Then keep the energy moving forward.

And even with a plan, things will break. People will miss. But performance gaps don't fix themselves. And blaming someone for drowning when you never threw a rope? That's negligence — and it's on you.

Cut The Guesswork: You're Not A Mindreader

People aren't spreadsheets. They're brilliant, unpredictable, and dragging blind spots, baggage, and battles you can't see. They come with histories, hang-ups, and hidden landmines that don't fit neatly into an playbook or formula. So when someone's off their game, your job isn't to throw darts and pray one sticks. Your job is to get ruthless with clarity.

Accountability starts with honesty. What's actually going on? Under-skilled? Overwhelmed? Unmotivated? Because lobbing solutions at symptoms is like plastering a cracked foundation and calling it architecture. Looks solid — right up until it isn't.

You're not a psychic. So stop assuming. Start asking — because anything less than truth makes you a co-conspirator in the lie. You can't fix what you won't face, and guessing isn't leadership — it's an alibi. A convenient one, but still an alibi.

So cut to it: is this "I can't" or "I won't"? They're not twins. One needs tools. The other needs honesty. Both need you to show up.

And if all you're hearing is excuses? Don't roll your eyes — dig. Excuses are camouflage. Burnout in disguise. Fear in a hoodie. Sometimes it's insecurity. Sometimes it's survival mode. But it's always a signal. That's your cue to challenge the silence. Reset the standard. Draw the line where it belongs.

You want alignment? Clear the fog first. You can't lead someone out of the dark if you're too scared to flip on the light. Grab the damn flashlight — or quit pretending you're leading.

Before, During, and After

Accountability isn't a license to sling blame like it's free swag at a bad mixer. It's not an excuse to shame. It's a cue to partner — to roll up your sleeves, call it out, and fix it.

And don't confuse *having the conversation* with earning your stripes — you haven't. If you're serious about closing performance gaps and leveling up, these three moments decide whether you're leading or just playing boss. Miss one, and you don't just lose momentum — you torch your ability to influence.

Before the Talk: Prep like a sniper.

You don't walk in praying for divine inspiration —
you walk in armed. Be clear-minded. Ask yourself:

→ Did I set clear expectations?
→ Is it competence, capacity, or confusion?
→ Did I set them up to succeed?

You don't get to hold people accountable for what
you haven't made clear.

During the Talk: Dig like a surgeon.

This isn't your monologue — or your rehearsal. Your
job? Hunt for the truth. Then listen.

→ What's in their way?
→ What do they need that they're not getting?
→ What's been swept under the rug?

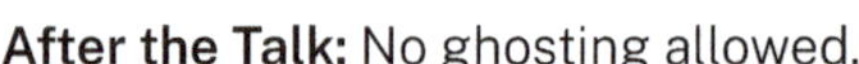
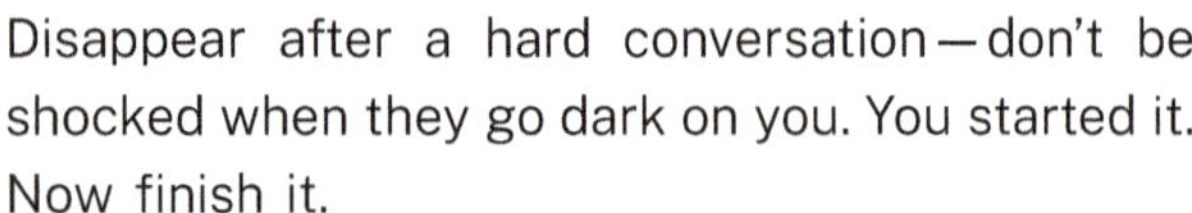

Keep pulling threads until you find the root — not
just the symptoms.

After the Talk: No ghosting allowed.

Disappear after a hard conversation — don't be
shocked when they go dark on you. You started it.
Now finish it.

→ Document and clarify the who, what, when,
  and how.
→ If the ball drops, call it, coach it, correct it.
→ The goal isn't control — it's momentum.

Leaders don't drop hard facts and walk away —
they stay until the message takes root.

This is the real work. Bold leadership doesn't dance around dysfunction — it drags it into the light and says,

"We fix it here — or we fracture."

No Exit Leadership

This is where the rubber meets the road. Accountability isn't voluntary. It's not a seasonal flavor you can drop when it gets inconvenient. It's the force that keeps your team standing when all hell breaks loose. So stop dodging it like it's radioactive.

Own it. The awkward conversations. The right-hook moments that test your spine. These aren't ambushes to dodge — they're testing your leadership to see if it will hold or fold. Skip them and you're just propping up a slow slide into mediocrity.

If you're ready to build a team that stands tall, fights hard, and owns their lane like their name's on the building, model it. Lead like accountability isn't punishment — it's your signature move, where mistakes become lessons and challenges turn into accelerators.

The way to get buy-in? Show them what it looks like to stare down the mess and say, "This one's mine. Let's fix it."

> Truth.
> Conviction.
> Follow-through.

Those are the non-negotiables. Duck the hard stuff, and your team will follow you straight into average. They'll only climb as high as the bar you set — so set it high enough that mediocrity gets a nosebleed.

And don't kid yourself — they're watching. Show them more than a title. Show them who you are. Not just when it's easy. History's already crowded with leaders who chose easy. The world's starving for someone willing to walk straight into the discomfort and plant their flag in the dirt.

> Own the mess — especially when it's yours.
> Carry the weight — before it crushes your team.
> Speak the hard truth — before silence rots the room.
> Take the hit — so the mission doesn't.

Because the only thing more dangerous than discomfort?

A leader too scared to face it.

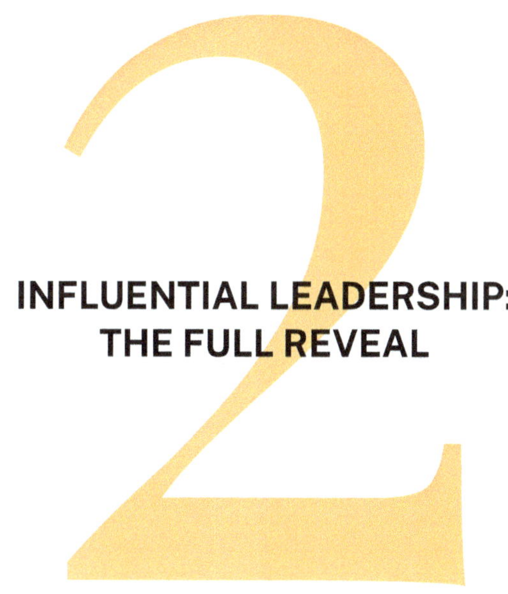

INFLUENTIAL LEADERSHIP:
THE FULL REVEAL

08

CHAPTER

Naked Frontier

WHERE LIMITS END AND THE FUTURE BEGINS

"Think small, you get compliance. Think bold, you spark revolutions."

MONA VOGELE

Lead Or Be Led

You're standing on the edge of the map. The safe routes are behind you; the unknown is dead ahead. That's the Naked Frontier — where leaders don't inherit the future, they build it. Where bold isn't a personality trait; it's fuel for a leadership vision that refuses to be a tagline.

Your vision isn't marketing glitter the comms team sprinkles into a slide deck to make shareholders wag their tails. No — a real vision is a war cry. It's oxygen when the room's filling up with smoke. When the world tries to convince you to quit, vision is the battle-tested blueprint that drags you back to why you started in the first place. It doesn't whisper — it screams, "We're not done yet!"

It's not cute. It's not curated for LinkedIn likes. Vision is visceral. Strip it away, and leadership is just a blind sprint into the abyss — another B-movie apocalypse with no plot, no survivors, and definitely no hero.

Sure, you could fake your way through the first few scenes, maybe even score a pity clap. But without vision, you're improvising yourself into irrelevance — and the final curtain is coming fast.

So what does vision actually look like? It looks like a young woman in a testosterone-soaked industry staring down a system built to grind her down and toss her aside. Instead of folding or faking it, she tore up the ops manual, rewrote it her way, and built something so unapologetically bold it made the old guard choke on their bourbon.

> She didn't ask.
> She didn't wait.
> She created.

Not for applause — for change. Where others saw limitation, she saw an opening. That wasn't just insight. That was defiance, uncontained.

Too dramatic? Perfect. It should be. Because this is where the story stops being a fairy tale — and starts getting real. Let me show you exactly how it all went down.

The Gas Station Experiment

Picture it: mid-to-late '80s. Gas stations on every corner. Mullets defying gravity. Shoulder pads that could block linebackers. And there I was — twenty-something, green but gunning — marching into the "all-boys" club known as the oil and gas industry like I had something to prove.

No guidebook. No business plan. Just steel-toed ambition and a vision so lit it could've hotwired a dead rig in the desert. This wasn't a toe-dip. This was a cannonball into the unknown.

I took the reins at a local gas station — not glamorous, not headline-worthy — but it was mine. Five employees. One overflowing binder of regs that read like bedtime stories written by the IRS and a whole lot of "that's just how we've always done it." Yep, cue the slow eye-roll.

It didn't take long to figure out I wasn't there just to keep the fuel flowing. I was there to build something that would make the overlords of efficiency weep. A high-octane engine of culture, systems, and straight-up defiance in the face of the status quo.

Vision was the ignition. Grit was the gearshift. While others were busy playing policy patty-cake, I bet it all on one thing: people.

Let me say that again for the cheap seats — PEOPLE. The holy grail. The untapped goldmine. The thing that turns "just a job" into a mission. This wasn't about a paycheck for me. It was about turning a gas station into a laboratory of what's possible.

I'd had other leadership gigs. But that gas station? It was my first main stage — and I didn't just chase numbers. I chased meaning.

Sure, operational efficiency was the name of the game, and I hunted it like a bill collector with a deadline. But I quickly learned that real success doesn't stack trophies — it shatters the scoreboard and bets the house on people.

And let me tell you, as a team, we didn't dabble. While the industry churned people out like bad advice — 30 percent turnover in a good year — we stood at 10 percent. Cupcakes and gift cards didn't keep them; being treated like humans, with curiosity in their core and ideas worth hearing, did.

We trained like it mattered. We listened like the answers were already in the room. And when someone crushed it, we celebrated like we'd hit a pocket under pump three. Because when people feel seen, they show up in a big way. We weren't a team. We were a renegade syndicate. Loud. Scrappy. Fearless with execution. The kind of crew that made the impossible look like a Tuesday.

And yeah, maybe you're thinking, "Come on, all this... at a gas station?"

You're damn right!

Because vision doesn't care about square footage. It doesn't need a leather chair or a skyline view. It needs a leader with enough guts to see beyond the register and build something no one else saw coming.

This wasn't some cute origin story. This was war, baby — the kind that yanks you out of bed at 4 a.m., makes you uncomfortable, and says, "We're not playing small today." Not humble beginnings but unshakable drive — created when resistance collides with vision and it refuses to blink. And that vision? It doesn't waste time on Discord threads or hide in Trello boards. It's a battle cry.

And when it's laced with action? That's not just progress — that's tectonic plates grinding. The kind that leaves crater marks where excuses used to stand. When people finally start paying attention.

The Future at Full Charge

In 2018, Tesla wasn't just circling the drain — it was doing pirouettes on the edge of the cliff. Wall Street had its popcorn out. The legacy automakers? Laughing like rich kids watching a YouTube fail compilation. The production line looked like a junkyard with a pulse, and analysts were already chiseling Tesla's tombstone. The headlines practically wrote themselves: "Tesla's done. Pack it up. Nice try, kids."

Enter Elon Musk.

He didn't retreat to the executive wing or outsource the carnage to the PR spin-doctors. Nope. He planted himself in the Fremont factory — shoulder-deep in the grind. One pillow, one sleeping bag, and enough untamed conviction to make most CEOs fold before they even step out of their valet-parked cars.

He didn't lead from a distance. He became the epicenter. He camped out at ground zero, ripping through "production hell" like a sleep-deprived MacGyver with a blowtorch.

→ Simple? Not even close. He was troubleshooting on the fly and breaking bottlenecks like a man whose insomnia deserved its own zip code.

→ Tidy? That's a hard no. Elon and his team tore into machines, bent deadlines till they screamed, and stared failure down like it was an opponent begging for mercy.

→ Pure leadership? Without a doubt — the purest leadership we've seen in decades.

And what happened next is now Silicon Valley scripture: Tesla didn't just recover — it rose like a phoenix with a lithium-ion battery strapped to its back and left the industry choking on electrified dust. The same suits who mocked him? Now racing to copy homework off the kid they once called delusional.

> *"It was a very painful time," Musk later admitted. "I don't know, but I was probably a little crazy."*

Yeah, Elon — you might call it crazy. But the rest of us? We call it inevitable. Immutable. Irrefutable. Fate that no one outruns.

Looking back? Tesla wasn't the underdog — it was the street fighter held together with duct tape, debt, and a last-chance prayer. They took on automakers with a century of experience, hoarded war chests, and political connections that went generations deep.

What those giants didn't have was vision with zero brakes — the kind that doesn't wait for approval and doesn't slow down.

Today, Tesla's market valuation makes the old guard look like Blockbuster handing out late fees while Netflix streams the future. Bundle any of the top automakers — and you still fall short.

Why? Because Tesla doesn't just build cars — they hotwire belief.

> Belief that crazy is just code for "not done yet."
> Belief that limits are just fences begging to be torn down.
> Belief that the future isn't gifted — it's engineered.

And for the doubters, it's a reminder — mock, resist, stall — fate is coming, and it'll flatten you every damn time. This isn't a bedtime story for innovators — it's a loud hell-no to the status quo. That's vision unshackled.

So if you're sitting around waiting for permission, consider this your call to arms. The legends? The rule-breakers? They don't whisper their futures — they scream them into existence.

Now it's your turn. You've got a seat at the table — or a hammer and enough scrap wood to build your own. Figure out what your future is. Because leadership isn't passive. And this isn't a rehearsal.

What It Is And What It Ain't

Let's blow the smoke off this whole "vision" conversation and finally say what no one else will. If your leadership vision still sounds like a slogan off a coffee mug from the clearance aisle at Office Depot, you're not leading. You're just stunt-doubling leadership from the sidelines.

 **You want to lead with vision?** Start with clarity. I'm talking signal-flare-in-a-blackout clarity. Vision isn't abstract. It's not theory. It's the steel beneath the shine — the thing still standing when the branding glitter burns off.

And if you're confusing your leadership vision with your company vision? Stop. They're related, sure — but they're not the same beast. One is personal; the other, organizational. One fuels your choices; the other directs your enterprise. Get them twisted, and you'll end up with a mission statement that sounds inspiring on paper but dies on the front lines.

 **Your Mission Statement** is your war map — the daily fight plan. It's boots on the ground, sword swinging, no excuses — only execution. It's precise. It tells your people what's happening today and what moves the company toward its ultimate goal.

 **Your Company Vision** is the moonshot — the dragon at the end of the last level. The big, audacious someday that makes your competitors quake and your team's pulse quicken. Market domination. Cultural revolution. Saving the planet — or just disrupting the hell out of it. Whatever it is, it stretches the limits of what's possible.

 **Your Leadership Vision** is fire — your fire. Not the what or the where, but the how and the why. It shapes why you show up, how you move, how you rip open a path when none exists — the relentless force that takes the company's mission and vision from plan to reality.

When these three align, people show up on Mondays like it's *Friday Night Lights* — not dragging themselves in like they lost a bet. The company mission and vision get them through the door, but it's a clear leadership vision that keeps people locked in when conditions turn hard and quitting would be easier.

Without it? You're just another warm-bodied chair filler nodding through another email thread titled "re: re: re: Mission Alignment."

So forget the motivational drivel. Forget the awkward team-building stunts (seriously, no one wants to play human Jenga).

Your leadership vision is the thing that reminds your team exactly why they're here. Otherwise, you're dead weight — parked, waiting for someone else to tell you what matters. Time to get clear. Stop whispering your vision like it's classified. The mic's hot. The stakes are high. Lead naked. Lead loud. Or get the hell out of the way.

Vision Warfare: Leading Without Permission

Forget buzzwords, whiteboards, or whatever flavor-of-the-month mantra the C-suite slaps on a PowerPoint. Crafting your vision means peeling back the layers of bureaucratic BS until you hit bone — and dragging your real vision into the daylight. Who are you really? What are you actually here to build — when the masks are off and the heat's on? That's your blueprint.

And once it's nailed down, you don't just display it — you defend it like it's the last stronghold in a kingdom under siege.

Because make no mistake — your vision will get tested. It'll be mocked, torn, and shoved back in your face. Your job? Stand taller.

Jeff Bezos nailed it:

> *"Be stubborn on the vision, flexible on the details."*

That's not just a clever quote you'd see on a cheap screensaver. That's the battle plan. Because a big vision? It's not a sprint. It's a siege. It's slow, painful, and constantly under fire from doubters, delays, and your own inner critic with a megaphone.

That's when stubbornness saves you. Because you'll be challenged at every turn. And if your vision's built on convenience, it'll vanish faster than a parking spot at Costco on Saturday. It has to be an unshakable, unapologetic devotion to your why — the kind that holds the line when everything else breaks.

And if you're not willing to go full trench warfare for it, then sit down. You're not ready. This battlefield eats the unprepared alive.

But don't confuse stubborn for stupid. That's where flexibility shows up — swinging a crowbar.

Flexibility is the voice that says, "Yeah, that plan just exploded — but we're still going." It's pivoting when the launch flops. Laughing when the plan backhands you. Tweaking, shifting, trying again — because the destination hasn't changed, only the path.

> Stubborn vision.
> Flexible execution.

That's the lethal duo. The grit-and-grace combo that bends reality. Success doesn't waltz in wearing a name tag. It's carved out of the side of a mountain with calloused hands and heat rolling off you. So grab the rope. Clip in. And start climbing. Because the mountain's not moving. You are.

Time to Ink Your Revolution

Go back to the start — *your* start. Not the sanitized, PR-friendly origin story they could slap on a brochure — the real one you dug into in Chapter 1. The moment your archetype stepped out of the shadows, grabbed you by the collar — and something deep in your ribcage whispered, "You were made for more than this." And you actually believed it.

Bring that same version of you into this moment and grab your non-negotiables. Not the poster-friendly company values. The ones seared into your bones long before you ever had a title — the ones you'd go to the mat for. This isn't about following someone else's script — it's showing up with the authority of someone who built the building from scratch and moves like there's no Plan B.

→	Safe? That's adorable.

But safe never started revolutions, and it damn sure won't write a story worth remembering. You need a vision that makes your heart slam in your chest. The kind that feels like stepping off a cliff, parachute locked, with nothing but open sky and instinct. Because without a vision that unhinges the room, you're just another manager with a to-do list.

So how do you want to leave your mark? Maybe you're the talent-forger — shaping raw potential into high performance. Maybe you're the door-kicker — the one who doesn't knock, doesn't wait, doesn't apologize. Maybe you're the chaos sculptor, unleashing your team into the arena — not to see them fall, but to see them fight their way into more than they ever imagined. Or maybe you're the architect — turning breaking points into shockwaves of innovation.

Whatever your edge, it better exude your story. It should carry your scars, your sweat, your fight. No knockoffs. No pretending. Just the kind of veracity that wakes the room.

This isn't about chasing dashboards or spoon-feeding quarterly growth charts. Those are byproducts. This is about reshaping the game. Your footprint. Your dent in the universe.

The leaders who make history? They shred the scripts and scrawl their own in Sharpie. They break ground loud enough to make the cautious clutch their spreadsheets like security blankets.

So here's the next gut check: how are you shaking up the world — or at least your corner of it? Take the weirdness, the wildness, and the ferocity you've been told to tone down — and build a vision that slaps like truth on a bad day.

Forget perfect. That's for branding agencies and lobby wall art. Real gets remembered.

And once you lock it in? You're not just leading anymore — you're birthing a movement. The kind of leadership that doesn't nudge people forward — it drags them into something bigger than themselves.

You're no longer whispering, "Follow me." You're lighting a bonfire and yelling, "Let's do this!"

Grab a pen. Lock yourself away — stairwell, rooftop, bathroom stall, doesn't matter. Get quiet enough to hear that Chapter 1 voice again. Write it down. That promise you'll stake everything on.

REMEMBER

- **Anchor in Your Archetype:** Who are you? Go back to that the voice, the proof you were built for more.

- **Draw a Line in the Sand:** What values do you hold sacred? Brand them into your battle plan.

- **Define Your Advantage:** How do you create leverage when it counts? Talent shaper? System breaker? Rule reinventor? Name the edge you lead with.

- **Make It Audacious:** Forget safe and reasonable. If it doesn't make your pulse spike, it's not fierce enough.

→ Got your vision? Good. Now execute.

Goals That Make You Sweat

Vision without execution is an illusion. Be the leader gutsy enough to set goals that rattle your comfort zone before breakfast. Most leaders won't. They underestimate the power of goals, aim for "safe," call it strategy, and wonder why they keep falling short of greatness.

The problem? "Safe" doesn't wreck you — it rocks you to sleep. That's what makes it so dangerous. It's comfort dressed like progress. You draft the goals, file them away, and high-five yourself for movement that never happened. That's not strategy — it's self-deception gift-wrapped for your conscience.

Legacy doesn't come from playing safe. It's built by the ones unafraid to reach beyond reason and grab what everyone else only dreams of. This is about raising the stakes until you're slightly terrified — because anything less is just code for complacency. I'm not here to serve you another reheated, watered-down formula from the corporate cafeteria line. I'm here to rip the lid off.

SMART goals? Yeah, they're cute — if your life's mission is a spotless to-do list and a "meets expectations" box checked at your annual review. They're for people chasing KPIs, not shattering ceilings.

Specific? Translation: predictable, not powerful.

Measurable? Another way to say "play small enough to track."

Achievable? Shrinks you, like progress needs permission.

Reasonable? Just another word for fear, dressed for work.

Time-bound? Chases deadlines, confuses urgency with impact.

Look — it's not your fault. I get it. It's what we've all been taught: stay inside the SMART box and call it success. Believe me, I lived there for decades. Then I learned the truth — that box is padded with limits.

Leaders worth remembering don't waste breath asking, "Is this reasonable?" They're busy tearing down walls, asking, "Is this worth it?" If you're here to leave your mark on history — like I know you are — you go EPIC. Because greatness isn't found in a checklist, and revolutions don't show up on neatly color-coded timelines.

So ignore SMART. This is your permission slip to dream bigger — to build EPIC goals.

> **Empowered.** Not the buzzword plastered on posters. This is hacking a path through the jungle where no map exists, giving your people the machete and trusting they'll swing hard enough to carve something bigger than you imagined.
>
> **Purposeful.** The kind that counts isn't tracked on a dashboard. You're tracking the lives you've lifted, the ceilings you've shattered, and the limits you've wrecked. It's impact that echoes long after the metrics disappear.
>
> **Innovative.** Not some brainstorm post-it wall. This means stretching past breaking and bragging about the scars because they prove you actually went where no one else dared. If it doesn't scare you, it's not innovation — it's maintenance.
>
> **Courageous.** Not "realistic." Not "safe." This is you making the leap when everything in you wants to stall. It's choosing the risk, shouldering the ridicule, and doing the thing anyway. If "realistic" is your ceiling, congrats — you just built your own cage and locked the door yourself.

EPIC goals aren't polite. They don't whisper from the sidelines. They stretch you. They don't box you in — they're wide open, built to move anywhere your vision dares to go. They're not built to keep you compliant or consensus-friendly. They exist to break something — in you, around you, ahead of you — and force you to rebuild stronger.

World-changing leaders don't simply "set" goals. They declare war on mediocrity. They lock onto targets so audacious they make the safe crowd sweat through their collared shirts. Wild, out of reach, unapologetic — that's what makes them worth the sacrifice.

So raise the bar. Build EPIC goals that don't just grow you — they reinvent you. Because if you're not at least a little rattled, you're not building a legacy — you're just faking ambition.

Ambition or Errands — Pick a Side

Anyone can scribble a goal on a Post-it and call it ambition. That's kindergarten hustle — arts and crafts with a side of delusion. You're not here to play motivational Mad Libs or stack clichés on your vision board. You're here to shatter limits, silence the forgettable, and make comfort disappear in your wake.

Now, setting the goal? That's the easy part. Ink dries fast. Commitment doesn't. Living it when your body's wrecked, your inbox is a war zone, and your brain is contemplating every escape hatch it can pry open? That's where your mettle is tested. Where leaders either walk out sharpened — or get flattened into footnotes nobody bothers to read.

EPIC goals aren't just time commitments — they're character assassins. They strip you to the bone, torch your excuses, and dare you to rise anyway. It's Everest without an oxygen mask — every step a bet against gravity, every breath agony. And somehow, it's still possible — if you refuse to quit.

You don't win by hurling blind hustle at the wall. You win by stacking small wins with surgical precision and by keeping your "why" front and center like it's branded on your forearm.

Comfort zones are just velvet coffins. The second you feel safe, you've stopped growing. No growth means decay — and decay makes you disposable.

REMEMBER

SMART goals are for clipboard warriors chasing progress reports and polite applause. **EPIC goals are for mercenaries** — leaders who didn't come to maintain but to set goals that split you open and rebuild you stronger. Anything less than EPIC is just errands in ambition's clothes.

Igniting Ambition In Your Team

If you're the spark, your team better be the blaze that makes the skyline glow. You're not here to chase dreams solo while they clock in, zone out, and coast. You're here to build a culture that pulverizes "good enough" and leaves nothing but dust. Dead weight doesn't get a seat at your table. Not on your team's worst day. Definitely not on their best.

And that's the thing about leadership — it's not about lighting fires *under* people; it's about lighting fires *within* people. You want them burning so bright the competition has to shade their eyes.

So forget the laminated five-point plans. Dare them to chase epic goals instead — the kind that makes them spit their coffee back in the cup and mutter, 'Wait…what?' The kind that twists their gut just enough — half terror, half adrenaline — because they know things are about to get real. Then arm them for the fight with tools tough enough to break through obstacles, and a space wide enough to sprint, stumble, and fail forward without being crucified for it. Because when failure's safe, growth gets loud.

And paint the future like it's a mural across the sky. Make it so visceral they don't just see it — they taste it. They feel it. They let it live in their core, not just their inbox. Every meeting, every decision, every late-night grind should pulse with it.

And when they swing and miss? Celebrate the swing. When they connect? Shake the walls with the win. Turn peer recognition into your underground currency. Yeah, praise from the top feels good — but when someone shoulder-to-shoulder looks you dead in the eye and says, "You killed it!" That's rocket fuel.

Never forget — you lit the first spark — your team turns it into wildfire. Make the future look so bold it shakes their bones a little — and makes them proud a lot. Then stand back and let "impossible" choke on the smoke.

Ethics: The Real Bottom Line

Goals without ethics? That's flooring it in a car with no brakes — you feel untouchable right up until you hit the wall. You can chase success at a dead sprint, but if you've cut the brakes on integrity, you're not leading — you're just a wreck-in-progress dragging everyone else into the crash.

History's graveyard is full of power players who climbed fast, burned bright, and then cratered because they treated ethics like optional seatbelts. The greats don't play that game.

Look at Warren Buffett. Grandpa cardigan. Gentle voice. Looks like he lives on decaf and crossword puzzles. But under that cardigan? Ambition with bite — and a value system welded in place. Ethics aren't window dressing. They're the currency that buys the privilege of having your name spoken without a wince.

Chase the top without that, and you're skating on black ice in designer shoes — it looks slick until the second it all gives way. And when it cracks, it doesn't just swallow your reputation — it drags every single ounce of integrity and every hard-earned victory you've fought for down with it.

That's the fine print of success no one reads — the higher you rise, the more gravity pulls on your character. Everyone wants the summit, but too many sell their soul for the shortcut. The real test isn't the climb — it's what you refuse to trade to get there.

The Climb Without Compromise

First, anchor yourself to your core values. Not the brand-safe ones built for optics. The ones that don't bend when the pressure's on or vanish when the money flashes. Make them loud enough to hit the back row and solid enough to stand tall when everything else around you is crumbling.

→ Then? *Live them out loud.*

Because your team's not memorizing your speeches — they're clocking your moves. When the moment comes, they'll remember what you did when it counted, not what you said for applause.

Second — get serious about accountability. Set up systems where honesty isn't a PR stunt — it's the baseline. Build a culture where calling out BS isn't risky, it's required. And before every decision, ask yourself: will I stand by it when it's written into my story — or will I be busy explaining it away?

Balancing ambition and ethics isn't about pumping the brakes — it's reaching the top without wrecking yourself. Climbing is easy. Doing it without selling your soul? That's the kind of leadership people write books about.

Lead Loud, Lead Bold

The fact you're still reading tells me everything. You feel the pull. You're not here to warm a seat — you're standing at the edge of the high dive, toes curling over the edge, knowing damn well you're about to jackknife into something bigger than a job description.

This chapter wasn't a cozy fireside chat about leadership — it was a line in the sand. A shot of adrenaline for anyone bold enough to lead with more than a business card and a nameplate on the door. Because inspiration without action? That's just a Notion board with commitment issues.

So — it's game time.

Grab the vision you wrote earlier. Yeah, the one you've been side-eyeing since you scribbled it down. Read it. Now ask yourself: does it shake you? Would it keep you up at 2 a.m.? Hijack your thoughts mid-conversation? If the answer's yes — hold on to it like it's the last oxygen tank on the mountain. That's your tether when the hype fades and the grind gets ugly.

If the answer's no? Don't worry. That just means you've got work to do. Some visions don't come charging in like lions — they stalk you from the shadows, waiting to see if you're daring enough to chase them. So chase. Wrestle. Drag it into the light until it roars back. Because a stubborn vision isn't a dead one — it's just testing your fight.

Then, set EPIC goals so audacious they make your chest tighten and your inner critic start filing HR complaints. Goals that don't just grow you — they gut-check you. Then hunt them like hell. Own the wins. Drag the wipeouts behind you like trophies. And when the breakthroughs come flying in? Don't duck — meet them head-on with a smirk and say, "Took you long enough."

Because this ride — this jagged, unpredictable, no-handrails ride — is yours if you're brave enough to take it. Break the mold. Pulverize "what if" until it's nothing but shards of "watch me." Then pen your legacy in ink so bold it bleeds through the page.

Because this is the part they'll talk about.

Make it worth repeating.

Naked Reckoning

WHERE HESITATION ENDS AND LEADERSHIP BEGINS

"Change doesn't wait for your permission—it strips you down to what's real—and that's where fearless is born."

MONA VOGELE

When The Skies Fell Silent

The sky that September morning was holding its breath—too quiet, too still, like it knew something the rest of us didn't. As I drove into work at Dallas Love Field, the radio started spitting out news that sounded more like a plotline for the next Michael Bay movie. A plane. The World Trade Center.

By the time I parked, a second one hit. Everything tilted, and there I was—a few months into a new leadership role at Southwest Airlines—watching the world unravel.

Flights grounded. Love Field—usually humming with that restless airport heartbeat—stood still. Silence had weight that day. It pressed against the glass. It seeped through the concrete. It wrapped around every passenger's stare—desperate for answers we didn't have.

But leadership isn't always about answers; it's about presence. Standing there, steady as steel, because your people need an anchor. That's what we tried to be—even though inside, we were just as scared as they were.

Then, the call came in—someone grabbed the mic: every Southwest plane, crew member, and passenger—safe. The room cracked open. Cheers. Tears. Relief flooding every square inch of that terminal.

But relief evaporated fast. We still had stranded passengers, security protocols to reinvent, and an entire industry to drag back to its feet. In that moment, leadership wasn't about speeches. It was about standing nose to nose with your people and making it crystal clear: we're in this together—all the way through.

In the days and weeks that followed, fear spread. If everything was changing, what would that mean for us? Then came the moment that turned crisis into a culture-defining story. While other airlines reached for the layoff axe, our CEO, Jim Parker, stepped up with one message that shot through every hangar, every cockpit, every ticket counter: our jobs were safe and our paychecks would keep coming. No spin. Just fear shown the door.

That clarity became our compass. We bunked in the airport, ran shifts around the clock, and grabbed sleep where we could. Nobody coasted. We showed up like survival meant keeping the heartbeat of our airline alive — and that heartbeat carried us back into the sky. Southwest became the first airline to fly again, not because we were lucky but because a tribe of warriors refused to stay grounded, flipping the bird to adversity and daring it to swing again.

What 9/11 burned into me is this: disaster doesn't always strike the way you expect. But every crisis leaves the same footprint. It doesn't shape leaders — it exposes them. Titles don't make you rise — they just put you in first class when the engines fail. What you do with that responsibility is up to you.

The Unexpected Leader

Crisis doesn't hit politely — it sucker-punches. Sometimes it levels an industry. Sometimes it blindsides you personally. But the defining ones come in hot — like a flock of geese slamming both engines right after takeoff. One second you're climbing. The next, you're aiming for the Hudson praying for a miracle. And in that freefall, unexpected leaders rise.

On January 15, 2009, US Airways Flight 1549 revealed an unscripted moment of leadership — rare, profound, impossible to rehearse. Not just from the cockpit — though Captain Sully's place in history is unshakable.

This one's about Dave Sanderson — a regular passenger who planted himself at the exit door, icy water flooding in, becoming the human handrail strangers clung to on their way to safety. Why? Because people were drowning in fear, and there was no time for instructions.

That's what change — especially the uninvited kind — feels like: sudden, ruthless, and hungry to see what you're made of.

Dave's story wrecks a lot of the lies we've been spoon-fed about leadership. Credentials are nice, but they're not the requirement. Presence is. In a crisis, it's the one person who doesn't move — steady in the chaos while everyone else breaks for the exit.

There were probably a few big titles and corner-office résumés on board. But titles don't matter when metal hits water. What mattered was Dave — the last passenger off the plane, risking his own life to help strangers out of a sinking fuselage. No prep. No guarantees. Just a man meeting the unknown with a steady hand.

As Dave himself says,

> *"You just need to bring certainty when everything feels uncertain."*

That's the job.

Leading through change — crisis-level or the everyday kind — isn't just about answers; it's about action. You don't wait for permission. You hold the line. You show up — scared, unsure — and still, you show up, carrying others through the uncertainty.

Dave didn't know the outcome. Most leaders don't. But he knew this: do what you can with what you've got. That's not a soundbite — that's the kind of moment that brands itself into memory.

And when change comes for you — and it will — you don't need a perfect plan. You need enough certainty to get your team through the next breath, the next step, the next landing. That's leadership when the water's rising and everything's on the line — the kind people never forget.

Mastering The Dynamics Of Change

When change hits hard, it doesn't ask permission. One day you're steady — the next, the world you knew is gone. 9/11 proved that a single sunrise can rewrite an entire industry.

COVID didn't just prove it — it carpet-bombed the world and left no corner untouched. In a blink, industries evaporated. Offices went dark. Normal wasn't just gone — it was buried. Adaptation wasn't a strategy — it was oxygen. And the survivors? They didn't just adapt. They ripped the wiring out and rewrote how business breathes.

Take Zoom. They didn't tiptoe through the COVID shutdowns — they erupted into relevance. Overnight, they became the oxygen mask strapped onto a world gasping to stay connected.

Forget business-as-usual — Zoom went from punchline to lifeline overnight. One second, they were the app you used when WebEx failed; the next, they were the duct tape holding the planet together — meetings, classrooms, happy hours — patched across overloaded servers. And they made it look easy.

Zoom didn't just pivot. They propelled. Daily users went from ten million to 300 million in what felt like a single refresh. No grace period. No garage to tinker in. They had to stick the landing with the world watching. Adapting wasn't just survival. It was a conquest.

COVID showed us with brutal clarity: change doesn't RSVP — it hits like turbulence before you can brace for impact. So start leading like Zoom did — before the chaos breaks — hitting every challenge, crushing obstacles like the invoice just hit collections. Not scraping by. Engraving your name so deep into the map the world has no choice but to navigate around you.

The Rent for Staying Relevant

Of course, not every shift comes at the scale of COVID or 9/11. Sometimes the hits slide in quiet — under the radar, out of sight — until you're flat on your back wondering what the hell just happened.

A supply chain glitch. A tech curveball. A competitor eating your lunch while you're still polishing yesterday's plan. They don't make headlines, but they'll gut your business just the same.

And it's not a matter of *if*. Those sneak attacks aren't waiting politely at the door — they're already inside, raiding the fridge, stealing your passwords, and changing the locks.

Most leaders today rank adaptability as the ultimate success filter — yet too many keep frankensteining dead strategies, praying they'll hold when the next storm barrels through.

The hard truth? Adaptability isn't a flex — it's the rent you pay to stay in the game. Forget five-year plans. Hell, forget five-month ones. The roadside is littered with leaders who thought they had more time. When change is inbound, there's no permission coming and no dust to settle. You either outmaneuver the moment and take ground, or you watch someone else plant their flag on your turf.

Owning the Pivot

Rigid leaders snap in high winds. Agile leaders own the shift. AI. Automation. Smart tools. This isn't sci-fi — it's already booting up on your desktop, streaming through your TV, and buzzing in your pocket. Ignore it and you're not just behind — you're roadkill smeared across the asphalt of progress. But used right? Tech doesn't replace your people — it straps jetpacks on their backs and dares them to fly.

Look at Domino's. They quit being a pizza chain and morphed into a digital juggernaut that just happens to sling pies. The Pizza Tracker? Voice-activated ordering? AI-powered customer insights? Domino's stopped selling food and started selling convenience, wrapped in pepperoni and innovation. They weren't reacting to the industry — they bent it to their will.

That's agility. Slamming into a new gear mid-race and maintaining the lead while everyone else fumbles with the clutch. No time for endless approvals. No patience for overthinking. You move. You pivot. You own the unrest. The ones who get this don't just adapt — they dictate how everyone else plays the game.

The Counterpunch

People don't resist change; they resist pointless change — the kind that feels like a corporate scavenger hunt no one signed up for. But even planned change rattles people. It throws routines into oblivion and wrecks comfort zones. Surviving any change takes grit.

And grit isn't about how long you can take the punch — it's how fast you counterpunch. When 9/11 grounded planes and COVID cold-cocked industries, the old playbooks weren't updated — they were shredded. Service was redefined. Operations rebuilt from the studs up. No one waited for perfect conditions. Leaders rewired the system on the fly and kept moving.

That's the gig. Change — planned or not — doesn't pause for your convenience; it's already on the march. Your job is to adapt and communicate. Some will follow. Some will dig in. A few will throw a full-body tantrum. Lead anyway — and flip that resistance into a catalyst for success. Because change doesn't feed on comfort — it feasts on courage.

Navigating Change

The reality? Leading through change isn't a joyride with your craft coffee and a Spotify playlist set to "vibes only." It's chess on a board that won't stop shifting — the pieces move, the rules rewrite, and the only checkmate is change itself. Which means your leadership can't play it safe — it has to hit like a Queen's Gambit, willing to sacrifice now so you walk away owning the board.

So the question isn't *if* you'll lead when the ground bucks — you'll have no choice. The question is, will you grip tighter, lean in, and make change your proving ground?

If the answer is yes, then here's your game plan.

☯   **Make Change a Growth Strategy:**

Change isn't the villain — it's the feral stray clawing at your door with a winning lottery ticket clenched in its teeth. It doesn't arrive clean or polite. It blows in like a riot, waving opportunity in one hand and dysfunction in the other.

Yeah, it's exhausting. Yeah, it drags you through drills you never signed up for. But inside that madness is your leverage — the chance to outthink, outmaneuver, and outlast every leader still clutching "the way we've always done it" like a pacifier. And the receipts don't lie: McKinsey says companies that undertake huge change are 4.5 times more likely to crush the competition.

So stop chasing "normal." That ship sank. Rewrite the rules in real time. Make pivots part of the strategy. Turn disruption into your home-field advantage — or watch your business get benched while someone else runs up the score.

☯   **The Lighthouse in the Storm:**

When the world tilts, your team isn't digging through policy manuals — they're scanning the horizon for a signal. One steady, unmistakable beam of light cutting through the noise. That's when your company's mission steps up. And if it's not locked in — louder than the static around them — you lose them. Period.

Southwest nails it: to connect people to what's important in their lives through friendly, reliable, and low-cost air travel. Not a slogan. A mission that moves. It tells their people exactly what to do when the sky falls — connect, serve, deliver. When people know what matters most, they don't panic — they pivot. So, strip it down. Say it out loud. Carve it into your culture's spine.

● **Mic Drop: Communicating Change:**

When the house is on fire, nobody wants a speech. They want raw, unfiltered reality. Deliver it — or hand the mic to mayhem and let chaos do the rest.

→ **Truth:** Say what you know, don't know, and what's next. Anything less is BS that people can smell a mile away.

→ **Tone:** Words matter — but delivery matters more. Panic spreads fast; steady presence shuts it down.

→ **Timing:** Silence isn't neutral — it's an open bar for fear. And fear drinks heavily. So speak early and often.

→ **Listening:** This proves your people matter in the mess. Ask, hear, and act on what comes back.

● **Fail. Fix. Repeat. (Progress is a Hot Mess)**

Mistakes aren't your enemy — they're the toll booth on the road to progress. If you're leading through change, you *will* trip. The only thing that matters is how fast you get up and how much force you bring with the next step.

Forget the PR-approved "oops" statements. Own the wreckage. Fix it. Then move. Transformation isn't pretty — it's cobbled-together ideas, scraped knees, and a graveyard of prototypes that died ugly deaths so the next one could breathe.

● **Complacency Kills: Stay Curious**

Curiosity isn't a quirk — it's a torpedo aimed at apathy. It smashes stagnation, drags you into the unknown, and refuses to let you decay in yesterday's wins. The second you start thinking you've made it? You're already losing ground.

The leaders shaping the future wake up asking, "What if?" They don't wait for change — they build it before anyone else even sees it coming. So stay hungry, or get buried. Because complacency doesn't build legacies — it buries them.

Make It Count

I think you get it — change rarely plays nice. It crashes in, rewrites the rules, and dares you to step up. Your job isn't to pray for calm skies — it's to grab the controls and make disruption your playground.

Because in the end, leadership stripped bare isn't about titles or perfect plans. It's about the moments when the sky goes quiet, the engines fail, the rules shift mid-game — and you still find the guts to stand steady, move fast, and carry your people when the ground gives way beneath them.

So remember — when the world tilts, four things hold the line:

> Presence that steadies you.
> Certainty that drives you.
> Agility that moves you.
> Adaptability that saves you.

And when your turn comes to lead through change — don't blink.

> Lead first.
> Lead steady.
> Lead out loud.

Change doesn't test what you know — it exposes who you are.

Naked Syndicate

OUTLAWS OF ORDINARY, ARCHITECTS OF IMPACT

"Renegades unite to build empires the timid only dream of."

MONA VOGELE

From Ghostship to Warship

The pitch was irresistible — smart people, cutting-edge tools, all the perks of leading a remote team without the corporate guardrails. I was ready to prove what modern leadership could look like.

What could possibly go wrong? Turns out, a lot.

Leading a remote crew? Forget the *Forbes*-approved fairy tales of virtual fist bumps and recycled hustle porn. This was trench warfare in sweatpants. Not your run-of-the-mill leadership gig, more of a disorganized hand-me-down — like being tossed the keys to a beat-up Dodge Neon and told, "Go win NASCAR."

There was no culture and very little cohesion. Just inboxes swollen with tension and virtual meetings that sucked more energy than they produced. The vibe wasn't unity — it was disarray, plain and simple.

Awkward Intervention, Epic Evolution

That first in-person meeting? Awkward doesn't even land in the same zip code. It felt like a group intervention — crossed arms, side-eyes, and an urge to bolt for the door. My gut said bail. But I stayed. And to break the tension, I cracked the silence with two questions:

"What's the vision — powerhouse or paperweight? And what's the move that keeps us from circling the drain like amateurs?"

Okay, maybe I didn't phrase it *that* bluntly — but there was no spin, no script, no brand-safe buzzwords. Just the unvarnished truth.

And that was enough to split the ice wide open. Beneath the frost — ideas, possibility, humanity.

Fair warning, though: if you ask for input, you'd better use it — or look like a clown running meetings for sport. Call it what you want, but that's a leadership test most fail.

Trust isn't built with polite nods and empty notes; it's forged in decisions, sealed with follow-through.

So I took what they gave me and laid it like stone — locked in with clarity and the kind of accountability that leaves no place to hide. The results didn't just work — they hit with the weight of a giant learning to run.

From Avatars to Army

Once the cards were on the table, I leveled with them. I wasn't demanding trust or loyalty. I was asking for a shot to earn both — putting the decision, stand with me — or walk — squarely in their hands when it mattered most.

The surprise was palpable; leaders don't usually hand over that kind of power. And in that moment, the energy shifted — everyone suddenly aware the game had changed.

Here's what they don't tell you about remote teams in the leadership offsites: isolation isn't a risk — it's the default setting. It doesn't creep, it camps. Communication mutates into a high-stakes round of digital telephone, where details distort and intentions blur.

And motivation? Most days it's flatter than the fake bookshelf you slapped up behind your Zoom square.

You don't need a spreadsheet to prove it. Remote work rewired the world — but for many, connection flatlined in the process, and isolation set in. That's not "The Future of Work." That's "The Future of Winging It" — unless you lead with surgical precision.

So we went full mad-scientist, fueled by dangerous amounts of caffeine — weekly check-ins, open channels, space for frustrations. No overnight miracles, just small, relentless moves until the avatars blurred into something real. That talented team finally stopped drifting in digital limbo and started moving like a pack — locked in, aligned, and on a shared mission.

When trust finally walked through the door, momentum wasn't far behind. And when the groove hit, it was undeniable.

Built for Impact, Not for Optics

So, if you're still leading for optics, buckle up — this chapter's going to sting a little. Call it a necessary burn. Because high-performance teams aren't born from slogans and pep talks. They're engineered — deliberately. What follows is the transformation: scattered to synchronized, lukewarm to volcanic.

Whether you lead 2 people or 2000 — across the hall or across the globe — the math doesn't change: trust, clear expectations, and execution sharp enough to slice through BS.

The magic hits when dysfunction's dismantled, trust is wired into the floorboards, and people stop clock-watching because they've got fingerprints on the mission — and they're playing to win.

So do the work. Ask the questions that crack people open. Build what your team truly needs. Speak with clarity even when it's uncomfortable. Then step aside and let them rise.

Thriving teams aren't accidents. They're built with intent, forged in accountability, and held together by leaders who refuse to settle for ordinary. That's where rhythm replaces routine — and harmony begins to rise.

Orchestrating Team Harmony

Ever get chills when your favorite band tears into a song? Not polished, not pretty — just untamed sound that rattles your bones. Suddenly you're fist-pumping, half-crying, half-levitating, convinced you just brushed against the divine. That's the gold standard: a team so locked in they could make goosebumps an official KPI.

But let's not kid ourselves — that kind of magic doesn't fall from the sky. It's built like a band on tour: note by note, rehearsal after rehearsal, knowing when to rip a solo and when to hold the groove so the whole band stays dangerous together.

And leadership? It's not about being the lead singer — it's knowing when to take the stage and when to let your team have the spotlight. Because a one-person show isn't leadership — it's a vanity act no one wants to follow.

The Rare Breed: Playing Past Expectations

Teamwork — the word plastered on almost every company's core values poster, yet rarer than a politician's straight answer. Because real teamwork isn't just about "getting along." It demands commitment. Discipline. Accountability. The kind of self-awareness that calls your bluff and dents your pride.

Harmony only shows up when egos drop, agendas disappear, and people step in for the collective, not just themselves. And still, most people get it wrong.

→ The Myth? Great teams are built by the "best" players.
→ The Reality? Great teams are built by the *right* players.

Here's the difference: the best players show up the same way every day — hitting their marks, keeping tempo, sticking to the setlist. And most days, that's enough.

But the *right* players? They do the work, hold the line, and stay disciplined — until the moment when enough is no longer enough. When the room shifts. When the stakes spike. When playing it safe becomes the fastest way to lose.

That's the test: do you keep playing the same tired tune — or do you step forward and blow the roof off?

The *right* players commit to a leap big enough to change history.

Moonshot Mentality: The Apollo Approach

Apollo 11 wasn't just a headline — it was humanity's greatest dare. A crew of brilliant mavericks pointed at the moon and said, "Let's launch a couple of dudes up there — and then, just to prove a point, bring 'em back alive."

And they did it. Stuck the landing. Flag planted.

That famous bootprint in lunar dust? That's the receipt — stamped proof of a zero-margin-for-error, live-or-die mission that made every other high-stakes project look like a school science fair.

Mission Control wasn't just a dispatcher's desk — it was orchestrated survival. Every "Roger that" wasn't just radio chatter; it was trust you could hear — the razor-thin line between touchdown and tragedy.

- → Accountability? Absolute.
- → Communication? Surgical.
- → Execution? So flawless it landed a movie deal.

The Apollo mission wasn't luck. They didn't *sort of* trust each other. They didn't *kind of* communicate. They were locked in — tight as a snare drum. That's not mystique. That's weaponized readiness — built on hours of practice, discipline, and the right players who flat-out refuse to hand fate the wheel.

That's moonshot thinking — people who don't flinch, don't stall, and don't settle. The ones who look at the impossible and start building a ladder. Half-stepping your mission won't make history — it'll make headlines you'll spend years trying to delete.

 **You want the right players?** Good. The tools in this book are how you build them. Use them without hesitation.

Bring it Back to Earth

Now, unless you're moonlighting for SpaceX, odds are your team isn't suited up for zero gravity. But you *are* strapped to deadlines, dodging chaos, and sprinting after milestones that keep outrunning you.

And while the mediocre teams talk about teamwork, the great ones live it. They don't crack when it's time to deliver — they close ranks, communicate, and execute.

The proof? McKinsey found that clear, connected communication boosts productivity by 20-25 percent. That's not a marginal gain — that's transformation.

Will there be conflict? Absolutely — conflict is inevitable. But don't treat it like a bad date you dodge in the supermarket. Drag it out. Flip the light on. Stare it down.

Conflict isn't dysfunction; it's progress in riot gear. Mission Control didn't tiptoe around disagreements; they wrestled every detail until it tapped out. Disagreeing wasn't a problem — it was the process.

Real teams don't dodge tension — they dissect it. They don't get petty — they get precise.

From Rocket Science to Running the Bases

If Apollo 11 was the platinum, big-budget production, then the Oakland A's crashed in as the indie hit that hustled its way into the record books. Two wildly different arenas. Same truth: great teamwork isn't about resources — it's about strategy, execution, and the ruthless pursuit of better. That's how you stop surviving and start moonshotting. So grab your helmet — we're headed into the dugout to break it down, *Moneyball* style.

The Algorithm: Outsmart. Outwork. Overthrow

Brad Pitt in a ball cap? Definitely eye candy. But the real star of *Moneyball* wasn't Hollywood — it was the playbook: a refusal to give in to the status quo, wrapped in rebellion disguised as leadership.

No all-star roster. No billionaire bankroll. Just a ragtag crew, a mountain of data, and a manager who saw potential where everyone else saw scraps. They didn't just compete — they won. Because flash fades. Precision doesn't.

And guess what? That playbook translates anywhere — from a baseball team to a marketing crew to a pack of overcaffeinated developers on Slack. Tired of hearing "We don't have the resources"? Then make strategy the name of the game.

Know the Players, Play the Numbers

This isn't about team building — it's your war room intel and your competitive advantage. If you don't know exactly who's on the field, you're coaching blind.

Don't just hand out assignments — diagnose talent. Strip it down to the studs. Who delivers when the clock's running out? Who sees the entire board, not just their role? Use whatever tools get you the intel — personality tests, skill inventories, even that weird tarot deck the new guy swears by.

- → The method? Irrelevant.
- → The insight? Everything.

Then put people exactly where they shine and step back. Watch productivity explode — like a line drive over Fenway's Green Monster. Not gradual. Immediate.

And don't kid yourself — gut instinct isn't strategy. The A's didn't gamble; they built a religion out of hard stats. Start tracking what actually moves the needle: productivity, engagement, consistency, quality, innovation. Who's climbing? Who's coasting? Who needs reminding that they were built for more?

And for the love of progress, don't bury the numbers in some VP's spreadsheet crypt. Air them out. Let the hard truth talk. When the team sees the data, they either rise to the challenge or step aside. Both are progress. Both serve the mission. Either way — you win.

Culture Demands Risk

The best strategy on Earth will still belly-flop if your culture's rotten. Toxic work environments aren't just bad vibes — they're silent killers dressed in business casual.

If you're serious about winning, ditch the robotic performance reviews. Start having conversations that leave people sharper, not shattered. Pick one focus — whatever's crashing the most — go all in for thirty days. Stack the wins. Small ones pile up into home runs.

 **You want innovation?** Make failure the ticket in.
You want collaboration? Hand them the mic.

When your people fear the fallout from speaking up or striking out, they'll choose silence every time — and silence builds nothing. Google's Project Aristotle made it painfully clear: psychological safety is the single biggest predictor of team success.

So eradicate the fear factory. Run no-limits brainstorms where wild ideas aren't just tolerated — they're celebrated. When someone swings and misses, applaud it. The message is non-negotiable — risk is the requirement. Playing it safe is the liability.

Range Over Replicas

Sameness is the enemy of greatness. When everyone thinks, acts, and works the same way it isn't a team — it's an echo chamber.

The A's didn't win by chasing clones. They stacked the bench with range. They spotted magic where everyone else saw wildcards — and turned scraps into game-winning execution. Diversity — of thought, of background, of lived experience — isn't the latest trend. It's your ace in the hole.

> Amplify every voice.
> Elevate the contrarians.
> Protect the unconventional thinkers.

Because echo chambers breed extinction — and if you don't break them, they'll bury your team long before the competition does.

This isn't about instant gratification. Building a high-performance crew takes patience and the nerve to keep swinging when the easy answer is to quit.

But when it clicks — when your "maybe" roster mutates into a squad you'd bet the farm on — that's the payoff. That's when you know that every challenge, risk, and hard call was worth it.

Unstoppable doesn't just show up. You build it.

Handling The Spotlight Stealer

Your team's cooking. Momentum's building. Then — bam — ego. One player steals the spotlight, and the whole culture wobbles. I've seen it derail teams, departments, even entire companies.

Case in point: the '94 NBA Playoffs — Bulls vs. Knicks. Game tied. Seconds left. Everyone expects Scottie Pippen to take the shot. He's the guy. The post-Jordan anchor.

But Coach Phil Jackson hands it to rookie Toni Kukoc instead. And Pippen? Refuses to check back in. Plants himself on the bench like the basketball gods had betrayed him personally. Yep, you heard that right. One of the greatest players in history benched himself — in the final seconds of a playoff game — because the spotlight wasn't his.

Kukoc sinks it. Bulls win — but the locker room feels like a morgue. That's the cost of unchecked ego: the scoreboard says victory, but trust takes the loss. This isn't a bad day scenario — it's a fault line. One ego-fueled move and the harmony you've built gets blown off course. Now the mission's on pause while you manage damage control.

So when someone hijacks the spotlight, you shut it down — fast. No letting it "work itself out." Because ego grows in silence, and the longer you let it lead, the more it eats away at everything you've built.

When Ego Dies, Teams Rise

Coach Jackson didn't let it slide. Team over self — non-negotiable. That's the move when someone goes rogue: you draw the line so sharp it leaves no room for interpretation. Collaboration is the ticket in. Credit is shared. Anyone who exploits the mission for personal glory earns the bench, not a free pass.

- → Greatness? Always welcome.
- → Ego that steamrolls the team? Denied.

The measure of great leadership isn't in your ability to prevent every meltdown — it's stopping what you can and leading through what you can't. Pippen didn't get erased. He got coached. Your people deserve the same shot. Mistakes don't end careers —

refusing to fix them does. Real leadership isn't preached; it's proven in how you handle the fallout.

Seasoned leaders know the real wins belong to the whole crew — the front office guy keeping the machine humming, the accountant making sure the lights stay on, the teammate who passed the ball instead of hogging the shot. They're all MVPs. They build cultures where victories are shared and glory isn't hoarded.

Spread the credit. Shrink the ego. Because the moment the "me" outshouts the "we," the game's already lost.

Once trust and talent are locked in, the team needs direction — the vision that turns potential into proof. Because even the best crew can't win if they don't know where they're headed.

The War Map

This chapter wasn't written to pad your confidence or feed you another dose of leadership cotton candy. It's not a pep talk — it's a playbook for the trenches, a war map for greatness. The kind that stains, stretches, and shapes you.

Whether you're leading an office squad, coaching pint-sized sluggers, or prepping your crew for Mars (hey, Elon — hit me up), the mission's the same.

Legendary teams aren't happy accidents. They're built — brick by brutal brick — by leaders who create when others crumble, who choose pressure over comfort, and who know greatness doesn't show up by chance. It's constructed, tested, and earned by:

Every standard you set.
Every boundary you enforce.
Every high-five you give — it all adds up.

There's only one way to build a team that fights through the ugly, thrives under pressure, and wins when the odds are garbage. Stop babysitting warm bodies just marking time. Start building with intent — every damn moment.

The blueprint: The Six Naked Truths.

Trust that doesn't compromise.
Connection that takes root.
Communication that cuts through the BS.
EQ sharp enough to see what silence hides.
Culture that lives and breathes.
Accountability that flips screw-ups into comebacks.

But don't stop there. Level up.

Share the vision so vividly they'd chase it barefoot.
Embrace conflict that sharpens instead of shatters.
Set goals so audacious they scare the quit out of you.
Celebrate wins like fireworks, not confetti.
Adapt fast and lead when calm collapses.

This isn't about climbing the middle management ladder — it's about architecting a brighter, bolder future. Maybe it's on the world stage. Maybe it's in your community. Maybe it's around your own dinner table. Wherever you lead, you're not just moving people — you're building a legacy.

And legacies don't stumble into existence. They're created by leaders relentless enough to tilt the world itself.

The Final Word: Are You In Or Just Watching?

You've seen behind the curtain — the naked truth of leadership, unplugged, unfiltered, and unedited. If you're still here, you're not chasing comfort. You're chasing leadership that outlives you.

- → The perfect leader? Doesn't exist.
- → The perfect team? Doesn't either.

The beauty is, neither is required to change everything.

As Steve Jobs once said,

> *"The people who are crazy enough to think they can change the world are the ones who do."*

That's music to my ears. Now make that crazy undeniable.

Because "that's impossible" isn't a red light — it's a dare. The kind legacy leaders take personally — defying the odds and rebuilding the world anyway.

> Lead without permission.
> Lead with conviction.
> Lead naked.

History doesn't wait for volunteers.

It remembers the bold — and buries the rest.

The Uprising

RISE. REBUILD. TAKE BACK YOUR FUTURE

"You don't need to change everything, for everything to change."

MONA VOGELE

The Naked Truth Hits Different

By now I'm guessing you're not chasing shortcuts. You're not here for BS or bedtime stories — you want results that matter. You're not just grinding for today; you're building a future worth writing your name on. And now you've hit the last chapter. No hiding. Just the final round, daring you to finish what you started.

But don't you dare exhale. This isn't the part where we high-five each other and ride off into the sunset. You're deep in the late rounds now, but the fight's far from over. No curtain drop. No credits rolling. You slam this book shut like it's a bass drum and yell, "Let's go!"

We didn't strip it down so you could stay soft. We ripped it to the studs to build something unshakable. Because out there, leadership feels like a gladiator pit — and you're done playing defense.

You've locked in the six naked truths. Each one's a tool. Together, they're an arsenal. But an arsenal alone is dead weight with delusions of grandeur. It gets you in the ring, but it won't etch your name into the stories people still tell decades later. Not unless you're ready to go full tilt, gloves off, chin up to every voice that says you're not enough — and build something bold in spite of it all.

The ones who last aren't minted in cushy boardrooms. They're born in the moments the world tries to bury them — and they dig their way out inch by inch.

Like them, you'll be dismissed. Doubted. Hell, they'll laugh at you for daring to dream bigger than the box they've crammed themselves into. They'll roll their eyes at your ambition, mock your tenacity, and label your courage reckless. You'll be underestimated by people who wouldn't recognize grit if it punched them in the throat. They'll snicker behind soft smiles, whisper in back rooms, and chant the same worn-out line: "That'll never work."

My response? Good. Let them.

Because leaders with audacious visions don't get cheered — they get challenged. They don't draw applause; they draw critics and doubters — too dumb to resist the heat of what they'll never understand. And when they fly too close, the heat exposes what they're really made of.

And you? You'll just smile. Because nothing rattles the scrappy ones — the underestimated, the leaders with dirt under their nails and rebellion in their veins. They don't play to win — they play to rewrite the game, leaving doubters behind, choking on dust.

But every fighter knows the truth — glory comes with bruises. You'll be tested round after round. Because when the bell rings, leadership narrows to one brutal challenge: rise — or tap out.

Cue the scene: the iconic movie *Rocky* — the 14th round. Apollo Creed convinced the story's already written. Rocky's down on the canvas — his face a roadmap of pain. Mickey's in the corner, voice shredded, yelling, "Stay down! STAY DOWN!" Even the universe seems to whisper, "Call it, kid."

But deep in his marrow, something answers — "No." Against all logic. Against the lead weights in his arms and the thunder in his ribs. Against every sane excuse to quit. Rocky drags himself up — slow, deliberate — defiance carving its way through exhaustion. Apollo turns, victory already stamped on his face, and sees Rocky.

Standing. Again.

And in that moment, everything changes. Because the fight isn't in the fists — it's in the refusal to stay down. That's the line that separates contenders from conquerors. The second you rise when the world expects you to fold — that's when you become unstoppable.

Built For The Comeback

The world doesn't need more hollow suits — it's already choking on them. What it's starving for? Someone courageously real.

It needs you!

You don't need all the answers. You need guts. The tenacity to show up when every bone in your body screams, "Not today!" The audacity to dream bigger when everyone around you whispers, "Don't bother."

And when they doubt you — I'll say it louder this time:

Good. Let them!

Let their doubt be your fuel. You're not here for their approval. You're here to prove what relentless looks like to yourself and the world.

You're Rocky Balboa, gloves heavy, eyes swollen, the crowd already chanting someone else's name. The doubters are sipping their victory champagne before the bell even rings. But you? You're that quiet rebellion in the corner. The defiance that rises.

> Not because it's easy.
> Not because it's logical.
> But because it's who you are.

When they think they've buried you — when they're already drafting your eulogy — you rise. Bruised. Unbroken. With that dangerous glint in your eye that says, ***"You really thought that was all I had?"***

You're not just leading — you're rewriting the rules. You're here to shatter the stale, root out the dead weight, and build something holy out of the wreckage.

It's You vs. Every Excuse You've Ever Made

This is it. No "when the timing's right." No "someday" safety net. Now.

Step into the arena. Build trust so unshakable it holds when the walls are buckling. Speak truth that rattles the room, even when your voice rides the tremor. Lead with empathy and compassion so genuine the cynics choke on their own doubt. Forge bonds that drag people through hell and back. Demand a culture of accountability — not with fear as the stick but with respect as the standard — because greatness doesn't negotiate.

Leadership will hit you. Hard. It'll rattle your confidence and leave you asking if it's worth it. The only question that matters is this — will you get back up?

Because the ones who rise? They don't just lead — they alter the landscape. The world is waiting. Your team is watching.

And the doubters? They're seated front row, popcorn in hand, whispering your defeat before the fight's even started. So, give them a show they'll never forget.

Stand tall. Swing hard.

Lead naked — not with pretense, but with purpose.

And when the crowd starts yelling, *"Stay down! STAY DOWN!"* you drag yourself off the mat, grin ripped wide across your face, and whisper — "Never."

Every. Damn. Time.

The Revelation

**THE EPILOGUE:
THE WALL STILL STANDS**

"Let us rise up and build."
—Nehemiah 2:18

MONA VOGELE

The Sacred Foundation

Throughout this book, I've talked about leading with authenticity and transparency — stripping away the armor, speaking truth, and standing bare in the hard places. But there's one more layer beneath all of it — the ground I've built on and the reason I keep standing when the road gets hard or there's work left to do: *my faith in God.*

Know this, I'm no theologian. I'm still learning — and have been for years. My Bible is dog-eared, my prayers are messy, and my understanding is still under construction. But one thing I'm sure of is this: some of the most enduring leadership lessons ever written aren't found in business books. They're found in Scripture.

Before God ever calls you to build something around you, He builds something in you.

You're not shaped in ease. You're shaped in struggle. The pressure that feels like it's crushing you is often the same pressure that's preparing you to carry the weight of the destiny you keep praying for. When God prepares you for purpose, He strips away comfort, pride, and illusion until what's true is all that remains. That's not punishment. That's preparation.

Sure, this world is starving for a leadership revolution — that's why I wrote this book. But it's also starving for a spiritual one. We don't need more managers. We need more rebuilders — leaders willing to walk into the ruins and put their hands back on what's been lost: faith, integrity, humanity, trust.

And for me, no story captures that truth more clearly than Nehemiah's.

From The Book of Nehemiah

Nehemiah was a Jewish official in Persia — safe behind palace walls while his people's city lay in ruins. When he learned that Jerusalem's walls had been broken for generations, something in his spirit stirred. He didn't turn away; he turned toward. He prayed for strength, made a plan, and stepped into purpose. And when he arrived in Jerusalem, he surveyed the damage quietly before casting the vision out loud: ***"Let us rise up and build."***

And they did — together.

Nehemiah understood what too many leaders forget: he couldn't do it alone. He enlisted priests, guards, merchants, and families. Everyone had a section of wall, a gate to restore, a piece of the mission to own.

The opposition came fast. Mockery. Fear. Sabotage. Every leader who's ever tried to build something meaningful knows that trifecta well. But the wall was rebuilt in 52 days — after generations of ruin — proof that when God moves through your vision, walls don't just stand; they testify.

Here's the part leaders often miss. The wall standing wasn't the end. Time passed. Nehemiah left. And drift crept in. Standards softened. Commitments eroded. Culture drifted.

So Nehemiah came back.

Because leadership isn't proven by what you build — it's proven by whether you're willing to protect it. Whether you'll reassert truth when comfort sets in. Whether you'll confront decay instead of explaining it away.

That's faith-driven leadership in its truest form: trust, community, perseverance, accountability — woven together and lived out.

The Leader In The Mirror

That's why Nehemiah's story anchors me. I see two familiar battles in it.

As a leader, I've wrestled with being fiercely independent — carrying the vision alone, mistaking self-reliance for strength. I've also faced doubt, resistance, and the temptation to soften the call just to quiet the noise. But calling attracts resistance. Vision invites opposition. And leadership demands you stay on the wall — even when it would be easier to step down.

Most of us don't get a blueprint. We get a nudge instead. A quiet call to rebuild something that matters. To lead differently. Not from a distance — but in the dust, with people, for something that outlives us.

When the noise fades and the critics move on, the question isn't whether you led perfectly.

It's whether you led faithfully.

Welcome To The Revolution

In the end, leadership isn't about reaching the top — it's about kneeling low enough to lift others up. That's where the sacred work happens. That's where pride breaks and purpose breathes. It's about remembering who called you, who steadies you, and who walks with you when the noise turns to silence. That's where real legacy is built — not in boardrooms or headlines, but in the quiet surrender of purpose over ego, service over spotlight, obedience over applause.

So if you ever find yourself staring at the rubble — the doubts, the failures, the moments you thought would undo you — don't back down — it isn't the end.

It's the rebuild.

Every trial you survived is proof God is still working.

That's your Holy ground. Faith doesn't waver.

> Whisper your prayer.
> Find your footing.
> Start rebuilding.

Your purpose doesn't drift — people do. That's when real leaders return and restore.

Today, the wall still stands.

> Because of purpose.
> Because of faith.
> Because of people who refused to quit when it mattered most.

And it's waiting for leaders like you.

Those willing to rise, rebuild what matters, and restore the world around it.

RESOURCES

Apollo 11 Story

NASA. Apollo 11 Mission Overview. NASA.gov, July 1969.

NASA History Office. Apollo 11 Flight Journal / Mission Transcript. NASA.gov, 1969.

Smithsonian National Air and Space Museum. Apollo 11: The First Moon Landing. 2019.

Bat 21 Story

Vogele, Michael D. Personal account, U.S. Air Force Pararescue, gunner and combat medic in the Bat 21 rescue mission, April 1972.

Hambleton, Iceal "Gene." *The Rescue of Bat 21 Bravo: One of the Longest and Most Complex Search-and-Rescue Missions of the Vietnam War.* U.S. Air Force Museum Fact Sheet / multiple accounts (2012–2025).

Zimmerman, Dwight Jon. "Lt. Thomas R. Norris and the Rescue of Iceal Hambleton." *Defense Media Network*, 3 Feb 2012.

The Epoch Times. "The Rescue of Bat 21: A Dangerous Mission to Save One of Their Own." 4 May 2025.

Blue Bell Ice Cream Story

Centers for Disease Control and Prevention. "Multistate Outbreak of Listeriosis Linked to Blue Bell Creameries Products." 2015.

U.S. Department of Justice. "Blue Bell Creameries Ordered to Pay $17.25 Million Criminal Penalties." 2020.

Additional references: *Dairy Foods, Food Safety News, and New Prairie Press* articles related to Blue Bell Creameries (2015–2020).

Bob Chapman / Barry-Wehmiller Story

Barry-Wehmiller. *Truly Human Leadership Program.* https://barrywehmiller.com/truly-human-leadership.

Bulls vs. Knicks (1994 Playoffs) Story

Basketball-Reference. *1994 NBA Eastern Conference Semifinals – Bulls vs. Knicks.* Basketball-Reference.com.

Pippen, Scottie. "Scottie Pippen 'Probably Wouldn't Change' Playoff Self-Benching vs. Knicks in '94." *Bleacher Report*, 10 May 2020.

Domino's Pizza Story

CDO Magazine. "From Pizza Tracker to Precision Store Placement — How AI Is Transforming Domino's Business." 2024.

Restaurant Technology News. "How Technology Innovation Has Helped Domino's Weather the Storm." May 2020.

Ford Motor Company Story

Mulally, Alan. "Leading in the 21st Century: An Interview with Ford's Alan Mulally." *McKinsey & Company*, 1 Nov 2013.

Edmondson, Amy C., and Olivia Jung. *The Turnaround at Ford Motor Company*. Harvard Business School Case 621-101, April 2021 (Revised August 2024).

Muller, Joann. "The Simple Management Secrets Behind Mulally's Ford Turnaround." *Forbes*, 2 May 2014.

Industry Week. "Ford's Alan Mulally and the Superpower of Connection." June 2017.

Former U.S. Representative, Gabby Giffords Story

Giffords, Gabrielle. "Gabby Giffords: Finding Words Through Song." *Harvard Medical School News*, 14 Nov 2011.

Morrow, Maegan. "How Gabby Giffords Used Music to Regain Her Speech." *Psychology Today*, Jan 2021.

National Aphasia Association. "Gabby Giffords Is Treating Aphasia With Music." 2016.

Gallup Research (Global Engagement and Management Studies)

Gallup, Inc. *State of the Global Workplace: 2017 Report*. Washington, D.C.: Gallup Press, 2017. Data referenced in subsequent reports (2018–2024).

Gallup, Inc. "Why Great Managers Are So Rare." Gallup.com.

Gallup. *How to Improve Employee Engagement in the Workplace*. Gallup Workplace, n.d.

Gallup. (Year unk.). Survey showing only 7 percent of U.S. workers strongly agree that communication is accurate, timely, and open. [As reported by Axios HQ, Herrmann International, Haystack Team.]

Golden State Warriors Story

ESPN and *Golden State of Mind* coverage of the Nov. 12, 2018 Warriors–Clippers game and subsequent locker room incident between Kevin Durant and Draymond Green.

Google Stories / Google's Project Aristotle

Sekar, Naresh. "Google's '20% Time' Policy. Case Study." *Medium*, 2023.

Buchheit, Paul. "How Gmail Happened: The Inside Story of Its Launch 10 Years Ago." *Time*, 1 April 2014.

DanaConnect. "Innovation Strategies: Unpacking Google's 20% Time Policy." 2024.

Google LLC. "Team Dynamics: Five Keys to Building Effective Teams." *Think With Google*, June 2023.

The Holy Bible / Nehemiah Story

The Holy Bible, Book of Nehemiah. New International Version (NIV). Biblica, 2011.

Houston Astros Story

Major League Baseball. *Statement of the Commissioner: Astros Sign-Stealing Investigation.* 13 Jan 2020.

Major League Baseball. *Press Release: MLB Completes Astros' Investigation.* 13 Jan 2020.

NBC Sports. "How the Houston Astros Cheated in 2017–18 MLB Seasons." 2024.

McKinsey & Company

How Bold Is Your Business Transformation? A New Way to Measure Progress. July 2023.

McKinsey & Company / McKinsey Global Institute. *The Social Economy: Unlocking value and productivity through social technologies.* July 2012.

The New Zealand All Blacks Story

Austin, Simon. "Sweep the Sheds: Not Being Too Big for the Small

Things." *TrainingGround.Guru*, 11 May 2018.

Human Interest Ltd. "Case Study: The All Blacks Rugby Team." 2020.

Lynch, Stephen. "Lessons in Culture from the All Blacks." Blog, [date].

Zilvold Leadership. "The Legacy of Leadership: Lessons from the All Blacks." 2024.

Oakland A's / Moneyball Story

McKinsey & Company. Diversity Wins: How Inclusion Matters. May 2020.

Lewis, Michael. *Moneyball: The Art of Winning an Unfair Game.* W.W. Norton & Company, 2003.

Society for American Baseball Research. "Moneyball and the Power of Sabermetrics." SABR.org, 2019.

Harvard Business Review. "Analytics in Action: Lessons from Moneyball." 2014.

McKinsey & Company. Diversity Wins: How Inclusion Matters. May 2020.

Patagonia Story

Chouinard, Yvon. *Let My People Go Surfing: The Education of a Reluctant Businessman.* Revised Edition. Penguin, 2016.

HR Executive. "Let People Go Surfing." 2018.

Southwest Airlines Layoff Story (2025)

Reuters. "Southwest Airlines' Layoffs Dent Its Worker-First Culture." 20 Feb 2025.

KERA News. "Southwest Airlines Announces Layoffs as Company Faces Turmoil." 17 Feb 2025.

Fries, Tim. "Elliott Investment Management Drives Southwest's Historic 1,750 Job Layoffs." *The Tokenist,* 21 Feb 2025.

HR Digest. "What Led to Southwest Airlines' First Mass Layoffs in 53 Years?" 18 Feb 2025.

Business Insider. Quotes from Southwest employees reacting to layoffs and cultural impact (Feb 2025).

Southwest Airlines Stories

Vogele, Mona. Personal account of leadership experiences at Southwest Airlines (1990s–2010s), including events surrounding September 11, 2001, and subsequent organizational culture evolution. Author's firsthand recollection, 2025.

Tesla Story

Musk, Elon. "We're Going to Be in Production Hell." *Automotive Logistics,* 2 Aug 2017.

Business Insider. "Elon Musk Says He Slept on Tesla Factory Floor to Suffer More Than Any Employee During Model 3 Ramp-Up." 12 July 2018.

Reuters. "Tesla's All-Nighter to Hit Production Goal Fails to Convince Wall Street." 3 July 2018.

MarketWatch. "Elon Musk Says He Had Long Hours at the Fremont Factory as Tesla Goes Through 'Production Hell' to Reach Goal." 12 April 2018.

Theranos Story

U.S. Attorney's Office, Northern District of California. *"Theranos Founder Elizabeth Holmes Sentenced to 135 Months in Prison for Fraud."* Press release, November 18, 2022.

"Theranos Founder Holmes Sentenced to Over 11 Years for Fraud." Reuters, November 18, 2022.

The Inventor: Out for Blood in Silicon Valley. HBO Documentary, directed by Alex Gibney, 2019.

Volkswagen Story

U.S. Environmental Protection Agency. *Notice of Violation to Volkswagen AG.* Sept 2015.

U.S. Department of Justice. *Volkswagen Diesel Emissions Settlement Documents.* 2016–2017.

Related research: *National Bureau of Economic Research (NBER)* Working Paper; Auburn University Case Studies on VW Dieselgate (2017–2019).

Zappos Story

Retail Doctor. "Zappos Pays People to Quit – Should You?" Blog Post, 2014.

Resourcing Edge / OneDigital. "Should You Offer Your Employees a Bonus to Quit?" 2015.

Zoom Story

Zoom. "A Year Later: Reflecting and Looking Ahead." Zoom Blog, c. 2021.

Business of Apps. "Zoom Revenue and Usage Statistics (2025)." 2025.

The Verge. "Zoom Grows to 300 Million Meeting Participants Despite Security ..." 23 April 2020.